Your Inner Will

Your Inner Will

Finding Personal Strength
in Critical Times

PIERO FERRUCCI

TRANSLATED BY VIVIEN REID FERRUCCI

JEREMY P. TARCHER/PENGUIN
a member of Penguin Group (USA)
New York

Jeremy P. Tarcher/Penguin
Published by the Penguin Group
Penguin Group (USA) LLC
375 Hudson Street
New York, New York 10014

USA · Canada · UK · Ireland · Australia
New Zealand · India · South Africa · China

penguin.com
A Penguin Random House Company

Most Tarcher/Penguin books are available at special quantity discounts for
bulk purchase for sales promotions, premiums, fund-raising, and educational
needs. Special books or book excerpts also can be created to fit specific needs.
For details, write: Special.Markets@us.penguingroup.com.

Library of Congress Cataloging-in-Publication Data

Ferrucci, Piero.
Your inner will : finding personal strength in critical times / Piero Ferrucci;
translated by Vivien Reid Ferrucci.
p.   cm.
ISBN 978-0-399-17184-0
1. Will.   2. Determination (Personality trait).   I. Title.
BF632.F45   2014   2014016116
153.8—dc23

Printed in the United States of America
1   3   5   7   9   10   8   6   4   2

BOOK DESIGN BY AMANDA DEWEY

CONTENTS

INTRODUCTION

One day a huge, rusty gate collapsed on a four-year-old child. He was trapped under its heavy bulk. His mother ran to him. She was a small, gentle woman, and her specialty was homemade ravioli, not weight lifting. But at that moment her son was crying with pain and fear: perhaps his life was in danger. She looked about. She was alone. After a moment of dismay, she seized the enormous gate, and with all the force of desperation, and with sudden, amazing strength, lifted it. The child managed to scramble out from underneath and get free. Later, to move that dangerous gate away, it took four strong men.

That child would one day be my father; his mother, my grandmother. In this family legend, who knows how much is true or hyperbole? Yet stories of great strength manifesting in extreme circumstances are well known and have been documented. In emergency situations, our notions of what we can or cannot do are reset to zero, as powers otherwise dormant are unleashed. I believe this to be true not only for physical strength, but also for inner strength. It is an essential resource. We may lose touch with it, yet we can find it again. It is right there, accessible to us if we want it.

I see this often in the workshops I lead. I ask participants in a group to relive a time when they felt their own inner strength. All kinds of memories surface from the past: parents who, having been abandoned with children by their partner, found the energy and spirit to bring up a family; people who had a financial crisis, suffered failure or betrayal; who became unemployed at a late age; who had a serious illness; who discovered their son or daughter was alcoholic or addicted to gambling; who faced the plight of emigration, or the loss of a loved one. In short, people who, as we say in Tuscany, had felt the wolf's bite—those times when a merciless destiny assails us and we feel bewildered and frightened and alone in an endless cold. And we believe we are not going to make it.

Yet it was precisely in such dire situations that these people brought out their best: their resilience and courage, their practical intelligence, and above all their inner strength. They felt a flow of warm, powerful energy that allowed them to emerge from the crisis stronger and more alive. As the Latin saying tells us, *Per aspera ad astra*. Through hardship we reach the stars.

For others it was perhaps a situation less dramatic, but one that forced them to develop a previously unknown tenacity. For instance, sticking to a course of study under difficult conditions; carrying out a project no one else believed in; saving up to buy a house; standing their ground against a hostile person; defending themselves against injustice or bullying. Reliving these experiences, they often are surprised to realize that their strength has never left them. It is still there, albeit dormant and forgotten—a force for which they are proud and grateful. Just remembering it, they are moved.

To be strong—that is, competent, centered, resolute, able to face difficulties—is a good feeling. To be weak—distractible, fearful, apathetic—is not. This is obvious. Yet who teaches us to be strong? Very often I see the opposite. I see people who do not feel up to their task, who are overcome by anxiety, insecure, even torn inside. Perhaps they are endowed with wonderful creative talents, a great capacity for love, or superior intelligence. But they do not express them—for lack of inner strength. They are like a small boat at the mercy of waves, like a man moving slowly and tremulously and making big efforts just trudging along, a shadow of himself. They seem to have lost their way, and know not even where they want to go.

It can help to understand the strength we already have, and that which we can develop. Inner strength is a subtle and intelligent quality: we learn to read reality in other ways, use new strategies, forge our character, retrain forgotten abilities, change the way we relate, and tap our own resources. More important still, each of us is faced with a basic dilemma: Are the events of my life the result of forces over which I have no say, or can I in some way mold my existence? If I can see that my life is not governed by factors extraneous to me, but is, at least in part, decided in my inner world, I will find a surprising new strength. And I will realize that this strength originates in a faculty that is too often forgotten—a central function, often confused with thinking or impulse or emotion, but having its own distinct existence. This function is the will.

Let us see how this is so. The will chooses between right and wrong—thus is born responsibility. The will allows us to risk and to renew ourselves; to hold a thought through time, and realize a project. The will enables us to face difficulties and hardships without giving up straightaway. It gives us discipline. It makes our relationships with others truer and stronger. And it leads us toward freedom.

But if we delve into this subject long enough, we meet a paradox: The will is invisible, and for this reason we have been arguing for centuries. Is it real or not? It is at the source of our efficacy and our every decision. It constitutes our identity. Yet we do not know if it exists! And, depending on our conclusions, we read the world around us in completely different ways.

If we believe the will is an illusory idea, then everything obeys a script already written: how we behave in each situation, how we live our life. The delinquent who has just snatched a bag has a faulty brain; the student with poor results has no future; how and when we get sick has nothing to do with us; the thoughts that run through our head are just electrochemical processes for which we are not responsible. In short, we are made this way, and that is the end of the story.

If we believe instead in free will, we have, to be sure, many limitations, but ultimately our life is in our own hands; the thief can decide not to steal; the student can learn to use the skills he has; our health will be, to a fair extent, the result of our choices; the thoughts in our head we can manage ourselves; our harmful dependencies and habits are perhaps not as inevitable as they seem. And if we are "made that way," we can decide to change.

Not to acknowledge the will impoverishes and weakens us. To discover and cultivate it can offer huge advantages and produce great personal and social changes—with one caveat: The will is not a given. We do not start out strong and free. Countless factors condition us: our genetic makeup, our life circumstances, our history, other forces unknown to us, our own brain. The will is a conquest.

The will is for everybody. At certain times life may seem unfriendly to us. We may feel it has awarded others, and not us, with the most desirable gifts: health and wealth, talent and privilege; maybe contacts in high places. Mostly there is nothing we can do: what is, is, and what is not, is not. Yet one element surely depends on us, and it is the will. Even if we do not have it, we can generate it. We can learn to use it to our own and other people's advantage, turn it into an effective and creative tool. What others seem to have received for nothing, we can gain for ourselves bit by bit—then we shall feel it truly ours: not a lucky gift, but our very own victory. Nothing can be more democratic. With the will, we give shape to our lives.

It makes sense to speak of the dangers as well. The idea of the will is often associated with clumsy effort, pedantic discipline, or bullying. Even with feelings of omnipotence. But those are caricatures. True, this is a risky business: like all effective tools, inner strength might be applied in vile ways or for foul purposes. Anything worthwhile carries dangers. Recovering one's strength, however, is worth a try. In fact, it may be an impelling necessity for many. We need not remain passive, fearful, and confused. We need not be fragile. Inner strength simply means developing the resources needed for facing the hurdles and traps we are confronted with every day. From my forty years' experience as a psychotherapist, from a great amount of research-based knowledge in the fields of psychology and neuroscience, as well as from the inspiration offered by the myths and stories of diverse civilizations, I feel ready to say that this urgent task is workable for everyone.

We understand what strength is when we lack it. A few years ago I wrote a book on kindness. At the time it seemed to me the basic human principle. For me, kindness is synonymous with love. Warmth, affection, empathy, generosity—all ingredients of kindness, together with several others—I believed to be the qualities capable of transforming our lives, bringing well-being and fulfillment to all. I have not changed my mind. But I have realized more and more the pitfalls of fragility—how impotent we feel, how overcome we are by difficulties, how confused and angry we get when we have lost touch with our inner strength. Without it, we are in a state of emergency. And then love becomes meager and hesitant. A balanced and harmonious personality is founded on the development of both love and will.

To cultivate inner strength is a goal basic to our mental health.

And it is the work of a lifetime. You will not find quick and miraculous recipes here. We do not acquire a new strength overnight. This task needs patience, and the humility to acknowledge our own weak points. In this undertaking, *inner work* is the way to go. No one is a static entity, and we can all develop potentialities we lacked before. This is a central theme of Roberto Assagioli's psychosynthesis: you will find references to him here and there, because various ideas expounded in this book originated from him. Ancient philosophies also talk of inner work: self-knowledge in the sense of reflection, exercise, and self-control. So do the Eastern traditions, which, as the way to self-transformation, recommend *sadhana*, that is, the daily practice of introspection and meditation.

In this book you will find an exercise at the end of each chapter. These exercises are based on introspection, visualization, breathing, reflection, writing, or concrete action. They are tools that, over years of work by my colleagues and me, have proved to be remarkably efficacious. The text and exercises together may be considered a course for activating the will. Familiarizing yourself with these exercises, and practicing them regularly, can bring insights, changes in perspective, and sometimes profound transformations.

The will is multiform. Each of its aspects empowers others. I have described them one by one in the various chapters of this book, and would like to illustrate them briefly.

1. Freedom

Feeling free is the number one prerequisite for health and happiness. We may feel captive to our own automatisms, obligations, and fears. Pressure from others may also oppress us. Freedom—or lack of freedom—colors every aspect of our existence.

In principle each of us is free. What we decide is our own choice. Our freedom is not a given, however, but must be won day after day. We can choose to embrace new ideas and new values, cultivate different interests, begin new activities, and develop new relationships. In other words, enlarge our range of choices or even radically change them. Are we up to the task?

2. Center

We cannot feel strong without finding in ourselves the place where tranquillity reigns, where we feel truly ourselves. When our emotions threaten to overwhelm and devastate us, we can find the center of our being. When we are subjected to intolerable pressures, in the midst of stress, in a nightmare predicament, we can retreat to an inner sanctuary where nothing disturbs, crushes, or distracts us. This discovery offers us a pristine feeling of freedom and serenity.

3. Will

The will is the central theme of this book. The absence of will makes our life tiring, bitter, sometimes impossible. We become slaves to others or victims of our own inertia, incapable of realizing anything we deem worthwhile. To rediscover our will is like breathing oxygen after a long apnea. We feel reborn, life takes a new direction, our strength returns. We have the feeling of being at the helm. Some say they feel more focused; others feel galvanized. What we will equals what we are, because through our choices we build our life, express ourselves in the world, and are known by others.

4. Plasticity

The capacity to give form to our existence is crucial, yet frequently underrated. We can illustrate it in this way: Imagine you are in a large, dark room. You have a torch that emits a strong beam of light. You direct it here and there, and from the darkness, various beings and shapes emerge—animals, people, machines, plants, statues, books, objects, and beings of every kind. Each time the light shines on one of these entities, it is illuminated, it exists; when the light shines elsewhere, that entity disappears. By directing our attention to aspects, interests, attitudes, and situations we have chosen, we give life to them, and thereby shape ourselves and our existence. Directing our attention like the light in the dark room, we call into being a new trait, interest, or activity. Or else we leave it in the dark.

5. Autonomy

To some extent we are all dependent and interdependent. But some are too much so. It becomes a way of being, and therefore a serious liability. They depend on other people, on food, substances, habits, objects. By doing so, they place their happiness in the hands of others—or leave it to chance. They live in a state of need and fear. They can be victims of blackmail and manipulation. The moment they are more autonomous, they can live a life that is truly their own. They are not obliged to trade their soul for an ounce of security or happiness. Finding autonomy means fending for ourselves. It is to discover in ourselves the source of our interests, tastes, and motivations.

6. Mastery

Our lifestyle in Western societies is based on immediate gratification. What I like, I want *right now*. This capricious impatience is typical of children, but also of adults who have never really grown up. We may let slip one word or gesture too many, we may act on an impulse and then regret it. It is hard to control ourselves and to wait. On the other hand, whatever we have no desire to do, we put off. A plethora of studies have shown that self-regulation is connected with self-confidence, health, and success.

To be at the mercy of impulses and whims is a dangerous state. Self-mastery is a vital goal.

7. Integrity

Coherence within ourselves allows us to feel more solid. In an age marked by a lowering of standards, sloppiness, and getting by as a philosophy of life, integrity is a formidable asset.

But it has a cost. We commonly find ourselves having to choose between what is easier and what is right. We can pretend it does not matter, and choose the easy way. Or we can opt for the harder path, the one consistent with our values. For instance, we may choose to help someone in difficulty, to look at a dark side of ourselves, to confront an unpleasant task, to face a truth we would rather ignore, to take an unpopular stance, to tackle a huge hassle head-on. Integrity is about honoring our own values.

8. Depth

In the state of permanent distraction that pervades our contemporary life it is essential to learn anew the art of paying attention. Too often we flit from one interest (or activity, or relationship) to another, in the same way we surf the Web or change TV channels. We stay on the surface. We can learn instead to concentrate, persevere, and get to the substance. Depth is will applied to thinking. Instead of skimming over a thought, we can penetrate and take possession of it. We dig deep till we find the vein of gold. To live in depth yields fulfillment. Why do we see so many bored faces, and why do so many people look for nonstop entertainment? It may be because they have not learned to make the effort to probe deep. This makes the difference between missing the point or getting to the gist of the matter, between being a dilettante or a maestro, between being bored and enjoying life.

9. Courage

Sometimes we feel engulfed by our own fears. As if it were our fears, apprehensions, and terrors that decided what was and wasn't permissible for us to do and to be. We fuss about health; we fear making a bad impression; we worry about impending failure; we dread losing control or getting lost. How many fears do we have? Usually we move within a comfort zone and avoid situations that may turn out to be tricky. As soon as we draw near a danger zone, an alarm goes off and we stop.

Risk, on the other hand, helps us grow and renew ourselves. It allows us to get out of the cramped space we live in and opens us to new and wider domains. It is a multiplier of possibilities. Are you ready to live a little more dangerously?

10. Resilience

Inner strength comes to light under hard circumstances. We may feel like giving up, but instead we find the capacity to start over again. The human ability to rise again after a catastrophe is great, and it has been decisive in our evolution. Resilience is to get up after falling down. It is the opposite of surrender. Above all, it is a different way of reading adversity and hindrance: not as unforgiving fate, but as challenge. Resilience is to believe that we can still manage, and strengthen ourselves through hardship and defeat.

11. The State of Grace

In certain exceptional moments we feel supported and guided by a force greater than ourselves. The boundaries of our being widen. Everything happens effortlessly, and with an ineffable feeling of lightness. These moments are rare and memorable. They can give us new strength and redefine our existence.

12. Odyssey

The last chapter of this book will be on *The Odyssey*. Odysseus, the hero, faces adversities, traps, monsters, dangers, even hostile gods. His companions die; he alone survives to return home. Homer's poem is the story of anyone who, through various trials, develops strength and intelligence and wins back her own self.

IN CULTIVATING inner strength we shall meet assets and propensities we already possess, because we have acquired them over the course of a long, stupendous evolution. For millennia we have exercised inner strength—struggling against all kinds of discomforts, enduring famine and risk of death, venturing into the unknown, risking our lives daily, attempting the impossible. Those who were not up to par did not survive. Those who did survive contributed to human evolution and transmitted to us infinitely precious gifts: the strength and intelligence they brought out in their tough trials now live in us. Paleontologists tell us there were twenty-three different human species. Only one survived: *Homo sapiens*—the strongest. Us.

We now find ourselves, however, at a critical time. The will that helped us so much, we have largely forgotten. To rediscover it again, and to develop the qualities we lack, is an urgent task for anyone facing hardship. But even in normal situations—when we work, relate, play, reflect on our spiritual path, or seek a meaning in our lives—will is the central pivot.

The will is an ancient strength, but we can also think of it as *new*. For two important reasons: First, because many original studies on the will are now available—as compared to just a few years ago. They give us a clearer image of it, free it from stereotypes and old prejudices, and show it to us in all its power and beauty. Second, because newness is an intrinsic characteristic of the will. An emotion can repeat itself ad infinitum. A fantasy, too, can be old. And a thought may well be overcooked. But an act of will by definition is new *every single time*; otherwise it would be a habit or an automatism. Newness is the very essence of the will.

To discover the will, to develop its qualities, is an urgent task for anyone facing ordinary or extraordinary hardship. But also in normal situations—when we work, relate, play, reflect on our spiritual path, or seek a meaning in our lives—the will is the central pivot.

If we do not have it, we cannot even get out of bed in the morning.

Breathing

Before beginning, a few words about breathing. It is possible that at this very moment your breathing is not quite what it could be. Observe yourself: Are you breathing with only the upper part of your chest? This is an anxious breath, which in most people is chronic and inadequate. A baby breathes from the abdomen: This is the natural state. Try it yourself!

Deeper, calmer breathing brings more oxygen to the brain. Studies show that it lessens or removes anxiety and depression, helps us reason better, and promotes well-being.

Breath is a unique phenomenon, because it is at the interface between voluntary and involuntary action. Usually we breathe unawares, but we can also breathe voluntarily. Breath can help us understand the will. To take ten minutes a day for correct breathing is an act of will that can give many benefits and make the rest of the work described in this book easier and more fertile.

Exercise

Sitting with your eyes closed, breathe deeply. Breathe always through the nose. Place a hand over your abdomen: You should be able to feel its movement, out and in with the breath. It is important to create in the body a sensation of spaciousness. The abdomen expands, but so does the back, especially the part below the shoulder blades.

Now, as you breathe in, think of space: a very large natural space, a wide expanse. Then the immensity of cosmic space. The images do not have to be precise and constant. You need only the thought of expansion and vastness.

At the end of the out-breath, wait a few moments before breathing in again. The out-breath is a moment of relaxation and surrender. Let your body decide when to breathe in again.

PRACTICAL HINTS

It is essential that you do not force the breathing in any way. When you are distracted, calmly bring the attention back to the breath. Be present to yourself while breathing. In everyday life, remember that you are a few breaths away from well-being.

FREEDOM

Breaking Out of Prison

Once upon a time a highly intelligent bird was forced to live in a cage.

He reasoned and talked like a human being; he was a true phenomenon. His owner, a rich merchant, gave him every comfort. He wanted the bird all for himself: "Where would I find another exceptional animal like this one?" he thought. But the bird could no longer stand being imprisoned. Day and night, he dreamed of freedom.

One day the merchant said to everyone: "I am off to India. What present would you like me to bring you?" Relatives, friends, and servants all told him their wishes. The bird once more asked for freedom—the greatest gift. But since his wish was again denied, he asked his master to meet a bird who was his cousin in India. He explained where to find this bird, and asked the merchant that he give him his news. The merchant agreed, and managed to find the bird's cousin. He was free, perched on a branch of a large tree. The merchant told the bird about his cousin. The bird listened attentively to every word. At the end he fluffed his feathers and, as if dead, suddenly fell to the ground.

The merchant was bewildered. When he returned home, he

went to the caged bird and told him what had happened. This bird also listened with utmost attention; then he fluffed his feathers and finally collapsed to the ground. The master was crestfallen. He thought his words had upset the bird. Confused and distressed, he opened the cage, took the lifeless bird in his hands, and placed it on the windowsill. Suddenly the bird revived and flew off to the safety of a nearby tree.

He was free. "What happened?" asked the dismayed master. "Without knowing it," answered the bird, "you brought me a priceless bit of advice. I played dead, and you gave me back my freedom."

—RUMI

It is easy to understand the yearning of the bird in this story. Freedom, or lack of freedom, influences every aspect of our being. Chains of any kind cause bitterness or despair. Freedom increases our well-being and our strength (more on the smart bird later).

At times our freedom is limited or wiped out. I recall an episode from my boyhood: I was in a lift when the electricity went out, and I was blocked inside the elevator, in the dark. It was an oppressive state. I felt that my desire to get out, my need for space and liberty, met an inert, impersonal, irremovable reality. It was more than a fright: it was a feeling of total impotence.

I can think of some examples. You are on the freeway, and you have missed your exit. You are forced to drive to the next exit, many miles away. That stretch of road is useless, yet you are obliged to do it. You are forced to go in the direction opposite of the one you want, and resent every bit of it. Or you are at a boring meeting, but your role constrains you to stay. Or on the phone, having made a series of choices from a menu, you are waiting in a queue, and must not hang up lest you lose your turn—while having to listen to the same inane piece of music over and over again. These and many other examples are of short duration and (luckily) of modest importance, but they are enough for us to understand what it feels like when our freedom of choice and movement is frustrated. To be sure, in theory we are still free: we could run away, yelling, from the meeting; abandon the car on the freeway and walk; and so on. But we know too well that these alternatives are unpleasant, impractical, or illegal. And so we feel forced, and that constraint oppresses us.

Now extend this sense of constriction to a person's whole life. Some people have the impression that they are living in prison, as if throughout their entire existence, not merely in a brief episode, their freedom had vanished. They feel their work, their family life, their rest and holidays, their day-to-day living and the way they organize it, even their thoughts, are all heavily conditioned and controlled. It is like being a piece of machinery that moves inexorably without asking for assent, and having no alternatives. It is hell.

We all have a deep-seated need to feel free. Any harm, any restriction to this basic need, may cause suffering—anger, rebellion, anxiety, or depression. We feel we are living a life that is not ours. It is as if we were riding a roller coaster that climbs and falls, turns this way and that, without giving us a chance to get off, just throwing us about like a sack of potatoes.

On the other hand, we all know the taste of freedom. To be free feels good—it is a deep aspiration of our being. We know that without freedom we are not ourselves. *"Libertà va cercando che è si cara."* "He is looking for freedom so dear to him": with these famous words Dante describes himself in *The Divine Comedy*. His whole journey through Hell, through Purgatory, and up to the pinnacles of Heaven is nothing other than the search for freedom.

Considering how much the loss of freedom makes us suffer, we could even say that it is at the origin of all our pain. Freedom is linked most deeply to our identity, because to be free means to be oneself: destroy the freedom and you obliterate the person. Only as free individuals are we able to manifest who we are.

Unfortunately, humanity has from time immemorial developed ways to limit or suppress freedom. Yes, we are contradictory: besides wanting freedom, we fear it—our own and that of others. Freedom means to be unpredictable, and thus possibly to make unpleasant, dangerous, or mistaken choices; to evoke ideas or behaviors that are incompatible with those of the social consensus; perhaps to create havoc. Some people prefer to be slaves—in one of the many possible ways of being a slave: they have no responsibility, take no risks. It is possible to forget about freedom and live in bondage forever without even realizing it. Not only does freedom vanish—the very idea of freedom disappears. But the unease remains: it becomes mute and opaque, yet ever disturbing.

The lack of freedom can be felt in many ways. We would need a whole book to examine and discuss them. A simple yes or no certainly cannot answer the question of whether or not we are free. It is a matter of various degrees of independence, and of different areas of our lives: We can be free in one area, but less so in another. We can feel constriction on the plane of action, thought, emotion, or relationships. Greek mythology, so clever at showing our pathologies through stories and metaphors, has much to teach us here. Let us look at a few examples.

Daedalus was the creator of the labyrinth—once you were inside, it was impossible to get out. The maze was so complex that one would have to wander through it for eternity, although a way out was, in theory, possible. King Minos had Daedalus imprisoned in the labyrinth—his own creation—because he did not want him to disclose the secret to anyone else. Daedalus perhaps would have known how to escape, but the sea all around the island of Crete was under surveillance, so he would have been caught immediately. The only possible way out was to fly. Thus he made himself wings out of bird feathers and wax, and flew away, free (his son, Icarus, misused his freedom and fell into the sea). Daedalus is the symbol for being able to transcend the self-created maze of our own mind.

Midas the king thought only of gold. Excessively greedy, he had obtained the power of turning everything he touched to gold—but the gift he at first thought was wonderful soon became a devastating encumbrance. His life was paralyzed. Thus our desires imprison us, and we are unable to see beyond them. We become obsessed, we see the world only in terms of what we want. The story ends well: King Midas was finally granted to find liberation from the spell. He immersed and purified himself in a river, which since that day glistens with a golden light.

Procrustes wished to fit the people he hosted to his ill-famed bed. If they were too tall, he would cut off their feet; if they were too small, he would stretch them on the rack. Here is the imposition of conformity—the unpleasant sensation of having to adapt to ideas and ways that do not belong to us; to be forced to live by other people's measures. Another example: Sisyphus was condemned to carry a boulder to the top of a mountain; from there the boulder would roll down, and he would have to carry it back up again. This is the coercion of endless, futile repetition. The punishment for Echo the nymph, instead, was the compulsion to repeat the last words spoken by others: the incapacity to express ideas of her own.

We could cite many more. But the freedom underlying all freedoms is the freedom of the will. With it we express who we are. Can we call ourselves free? In theory the answer is a happy yes. Freedom is an extraordinary achievement of our civilization. All modern civilized societies are founded on the respect of everyone's freedom. For basic decisions—for instance, the decision to marry—the presupposition of free will is crucial: "I do" is a choice you will never forget, and it had better be a free one

when you pronounce it! It is celebrated before society and recognized as such. So, too, for economic decisions: The signature
on a check, for example, seals a free choice by which an individual gives money to another in exchange for service or goods. The
signature on a contract is a ritualized way of affirming the freedom of the will. The same applies to political decisions; when we
enter the voting booth, we are alone. Nobody is allowed to dis-
turb us: no pressure, no obligation. We are free citizens.

A yes before a priest or mayor, the cross on the voting card in
the silence and solitude of the booth, the signature on a check or
contract: these are all ways of saying that our free will is honored
and protected. We can choose what we think is best. And we are
free to do so.

So, at least as far as our main choices are concerned, we give
enormous importance to freedom. It makes perfect sense that a
signature and proof of identity are often required. We are, so to
speak, *more ourselves* in the moment we make a free decision than
at any other time.

We take free will very seriously—and rightly so. If it is in
any way threatened, an alarm goes off. Just try to hold someone
in your home, to get money or sexual favors from another person against her will; to falsify an electoral result or forge a signature on a check or contract: all hell breaks loose, and rightly so.
To violate another person's will is a crime, sometimes of the
vilest sort.

But are we sure the will is actually present and active? The
existence or absence of free will is a central legal theme. Article

85 of the Italian Penal Code says that "no one may be punished for an act considered by law a crime, if at the moment he committed it he was not responsible," and specifies: "One is responsible if he has the capacity to be conscious and to will." In Anglo-Saxon legislation it is said that the criminal must have *mens rea*, that is, both the awareness that she is committing a crime and the intention to commit it.

There are also degrees of seriousness, which correspond to degrees of active will. A crime is gravest when it is premeditated and planned (*with malice aforethought* in American law: planned and with malicious intent). When instead the crime is committed without premeditation, or is marked by violence or hostility but with no deliberate intention to harm, then it is thought to be less grave (*second-degree murder* in the United States) but still a crime.

In recent times neuroscience has often been cited in courtrooms precisely as a means to ascertain whether, and to what degree, an act has been voluntary. The years between 2005 and 2009 saw a doubling of the number of trials in which evidence was drawn from neuroscience or genetics. Take the case of a fifty-year-old man who, after a life of honest work and exemplary behavior, began to collect pedophiliac photos, molested his stepdaughter, and exhibited an aggressive, hypersexual demeanor. It was then discovered he had a brain tumor that was pressing against the amygdala. Once the tumor was removed, the problem disappeared; when the tumor grew back, the problem returned. In his trial for pedophilia, the many extenuating circumstances were acknowledged. But he was not fully acquitted, as he had downloaded the photos only when at home, never at work: the impulse could not have been irresistible if, having in mind the purpose of not being found out, he could deliberately delay gratification in order not to be caught.

How much of our behavior is determined by the condition of our brain? Not an easy question to answer. The Royal Society has suggested that lawyers and judges take courses in neuroscience. In these matters we must beware of hasty conclusions and simplistic stances. This is a highly complex subject that shows how touchy, unpredictable, and multifaceted the issue of free will is. Still, for the time being, the basic old formula remains: for a crime to be punishable, it must be demonstrated not only that damage was done, but also that it was intentional.

Individual free will is protected, celebrated, honored, and acknowledged. This is what happens in a free society. In a democracy we are not subjected to limitations of our will, unless our actions could harm or interfere with other people's freedom and well-being. Anti-freedom methods that were adopted in the past, and are still enforced in some societies, were luckily abandoned long ago: torture; arbitrary imprisonment; excessive police control; the imposition of a specific way of life, habits, even clothing, food, music, and so on. This is a great victory for our civilization, a conquest we must never take for granted, but must honor at all times.

So, are we free? The answer is no—because all the constrictions that are no longer present in the external world are well and truly active *inside us*. Now it is our inner self that languishes in prison. It is a captive of prejudices, fears, and uncontrolled emotions. It is tortured by doubts and feelings of guilt. It is oppressed by the past. It is a slave of terrifying fantasies or compulsive rituals or erroneous mental habits. It is obliged to do forced labor. Maybe our will is absent, or undeveloped, or asleep.

This is a reality I see every day in my work as a psychotherapist. Each day I meet people whose capacity for deciding has been manipulated, humiliated, suppressed, or else never developed. Ironically, this often happens because people mean well. Sooner or later we all find someone who wants to decide for us. If we let that happen, we become estranged from ourselves. It is as if we were at the helm of a ship and someone came up to us saying, "Move over, let me do it." We are pushed away, exiled from our very selves, deprived of our own inner authority. Somebody else is at the helm. And we have lost our freedom.

Ines was a thirty-year-old client of mine. One day she called me from the airport: "Maybe I can go back on my decision." Her voice was weak and unsure, and in the background I could hear the noises and impersonal voices from a loudspeaker. Her flight was about to depart and take her to another country, where the man she loved was waiting for her. Ines had made the decision to go, and leave behind her own troubled family, people who had been intruding into all aspects of her existence, from her choices in romantic relationships to how she dressed—even to what she ate. In working with me, she had reached the decision to leave and start a new life elsewhere. She had overcome hesitations, feelings of guilt, fears. She had bought the ticket and told her parents. They had reacted with emotional blackmail, outbursts, and threats. But she had withstood the pressure. She had made up her mind. Now, at the airport, she was hesitating again. Scruples and fears assailed her like a pack of wolves.

I did not speak: I just listened. I would have liked to encourage her, to give her a little push, because that was all she needed. But it would not have been right to do so. The decision had to be 100 percent hers. In this Ines was alone. Had I nudged her, I would have taken away from her the very capacity she had fought so hard to conquer.

True, many people tacitly invite others to decide for them. And why do we have such fear of choosing? I wonder. If you think about it, it is a reasonable fear. To decide means to rule out: to give up everything except what we choose. And it means to open a world of new possibilities—perhaps beautiful ones— or perhaps dangers and mistakes. Moreover, responsibility is a heavy burden. If someone lightens it for us, we feel so much the better. This is one of the most intriguing paradoxes: choice is the chief manifestation of our freedom, and at the same time the epitome of our vulnerability.

Choices carry with them countless, often long-lasting consequences. They are like a domino show: one piece falls and knocks over another hundred pieces. We make a decision, and it can have repercussions for years, even centuries. Ines wanted to go to another country. She hoped to live there with the man she loved.

Maybe they would have children, who, in turn, would grow, make new choices, and so forth. Everything begins in a single instant: the moment of decision.

After the dramatic interlude of hesitation, Ines found strength of heart. She told herself that the decision was right, after all. She boarded the plane and flew toward freedom.

The great news here is that to be free and to decide is good for our health—even the small, banal decisions we make every day. At a nursing home for the elderly in the town of Hamden, Connecticut, researchers organized an experiment that became a classic. They divided the subjects into two groups. One group had the responsibility of making decisions: when to watch a movie, which plants they would keep and take care of, how to arrange the furniture in their room, when and how to voice suggestions and complaints, if and when to participate in a game with other residents. The second group was told that the staff would take care of every decision and do everything possible to make the residents' lives easy and happy. After three weeks the researchers took stock of the situation: those belonging to the first group felt better, were more active, and socialized more, according to their own and the nurses' judgment. But the astonishing results came eighteen months later: the mortality rate of the free-willers was half that of the control group. This study by Ellen J. Langer and Judith Rodin was then repeated a number of times and extended to other situations. For example, in the Whitehall studies I and II it was found that people in civil service who are higher in the hierarchy (and so have more decisions to make) live longer and enjoy better health than those lower down (who seemingly have less stress but fewer decisions and less control). In short, evolution has rewarded the capacity to make free choices. Those who know how to decide and feel free to do so are better able to face life's challenges.

Many people are interested in taking over our free will. For starters, those who want to sell us anything clearly wish to influence our will. Sometimes it is with just a nudge: the goods displayed at eye level in the supermarket are the ones that sell most; the artificial fragrance of freshly baked bread lures us to the bakery section. We are prodded in the direction they want us to go.

At other times the manipulation is more determined and dangerous. With the new technique of neuromarketing, clever sales techniques can enter our brains and take over our decision making. Thanks to brain-imaging technology, it is possible to study our reaction to places, images, words, and jingles, and choose the ones that not only evoke a more positive response but also activate the areas of the brain most associated with our sense of identity and value. When the logo of a product finds its way into the area of the brain most associated with our sense of identity, it is a winner: ever faithful and obedient, we will follow that logo, because in our mind it has become a symbol of who we are.

Our family members and friends often cannot wait to influence our choices. We saw this with Ines. It happens in ways that are more or less invasive, more or less aggressive: rational persuasion, moral blackmail, emotional manipulation, and conditional love are the main tools of this trade. And of course it is all done with the most admirable of intentions: I just want what is best for you, I want to save you, guide you; after all, you are too young to understand. Famously, we find pressure on choice among school-mates or playmates, especially in tightly knit groups. The punishment for not going along with group will is ostracism. Groups of all kinds try to influence their members' will by activating archaic fears. At the beginning of human evolution, being excluded from the herd meant being condemned to isolation, and therefore death.

And what happens if it is *we* who interfere with others' lives? What if we want to decide what is best for them, what course of study they should follow, which people they should hang out with, how they should take care of their health, how they ought to dress or which hairdresser they should go to—perhaps mixing the meddling with genuine affection? Trying to control the life of another is a difficult and complex task. We, the controller, will *also* feel straitjacketed, always wanting to make sure that everything is going according to our wishes. Sometimes it succeeds: more often it does not. But even the spurious success diminishes us as well as the other person. And it is always hard work.

Religions, too, may try to influence our decisions. I am not speaking here of true religious sentiment, of mediation with the Infinite, of sublime religious art, or of aspiration to the highest ethical values—the very substance of religion. Religion, in its best aspects, points precisely to the way of freedom. But in its most dogmatic and militant forms—such as threatening an endless hell for those who do not obey the rules, while promising heaven for those who observe them—religion takes charge of our will, even when it tells us we are free.

In comparison, the modern political parties in democratic regimes are much less refined, but, almost by default, they too are busy trying to influence our choices. In the best of worlds, politics means open dialogue, accurate and complete information, and free participation. But in the real world, politics often tries to influence us on the one hand with promises, and threats, catastrophic imagery; and on the other with lies—all the while making generous use of advertising to manipulate our decision.

Now let us look more closely at what a free decision is. Make the decision to perform a simple act: for instance, to take a deep breath or visualize the color blue. Be conscious of the exact moment at which you decide. Or think of doing the same thing, and at the last moment decide not to do it. To decide is not the same as to act, and it can also lead to non-action. How do you perceive the moment of the decision? Is it localized in some part of your body? Most people feel the decision as an event in their head, whereas some are not aware of any particular localization. The "fiat" of will—that is, the act of deciding, takes place at a single moment, even when it has matured over a long time. At that moment you perceive the decision as yours, as free: Nobody else has decided, it was not a compulsion. It was you—no one was at the remote control.

By taking a deep breath or visualizing blue, you have performed an operation analogous to that of prime ministers and popes, businessmen and -women, corporate CEOs, financial investors, and so on—though of infinitely smaller proportions. The world is shaped by individuals' decisions. One might decide to invade a foreign country or set off a nuclear bomb, or build a hospital and help the weak, or compose a symphony or begin a scientific study. Everything starts with a decision: it is what forges our life. If we feel it as ours, we know our life belongs to us. If we cannot decide, or we let someone else decide for us, we will feel alienated and powerless.

To understand the nature of freedom and choice, it may help us to study an extreme situation: locked-in syndrome, a grave illness that throws new light on the very essence of will. Patients with this condition, having suffered a stroke, are totally paralyzed and therefore feel imprisoned in their inert body. Take the case of Richard Rudd, an Englishman who, after an accident, was almost 100 percent paralyzed. With the consent of the man's parents, the nurses and doctors were preparing to switch off his life-support mechanism. But at that moment someone noticed that the patient could voluntarily move his eyes. Therefore, by his one remaining movement, he could signal his will. So they asked him if he wanted to keep living or not. Right meant yes, left, no. He moved his eyes to the right. He had decided to live.

I quote this example not in order to take sides in a complex bioethical debate that is beyond the scope of this book. I mention it to highlight the central faculty of deciding—even in someone whose every other faculty is disabled.

Another field in which the act of will emerges with great clarity is the study of brain-machine interaction. This experimental field is especially promising for patients suffering from paralysis, because it allows them to maneuver, by their own will, robotic arms that can perform movements and actions otherwise impossible for them. A thirty-year-old American, Tim Hemmes, who had been in a serious motorcycle accident and was left paralyzed, gradually learned to move a mechanical arm connected to a computer, in turn linked to the patient's brain by grafting. After a few weeks' training, Tim Hemmes had learned to move the robotic arm in various directions. The movement was not his, but the robot's. His was the decision to move it—in other words, the act of will. At the most poignant moment of this training, Hemmes willed the arm to touch his girlfriend's hand: "For the first time in seven years I could, of my own initiative, reach out and touch another human being."

As we know, there are various philosophical positions on the subject of free will. The issue of free will has concerned philosophers for centuries—and occupies them to this day. Are we really free when we feel we are, or is it an illusion? The opinions are conflicting, and I think the debate will continue for centuries to come.

Some people believe that freedom does not exist—that it is an illusion. According to this position, anything we do or think is not a free action but the result of mere mechanical interactions: It is determined, like the movement of billiard balls or the functions of a washing machine. In this perspective, I, in writing this book; and you, in reading it; and all those who hold the idea that we are free; and all those who hold the opposite view; the heads of state making their decisions; all of us in our choices in love and work—but also in food at a restaurant, what to wear, what to do in our free time—we are all puppets; everything has already been decided, everything proceeds by itself, in a perennial, unreal, endless pantomime, without a glimmer of freedom.

The minute we embrace this thesis, we find ourselves in a problematic situation: None of our choices, being necessary, has any worth anymore. If I choose to have a child, to cultivate a friendship, to go and live in another city because I want to, because I feel strongly about it, or because that is my independent choice, then I feel I am a free agent. I could have decided in any number of other ways, but I chose this particular way. On the other hand, I could read those same events as inescapable and having the inexorable certainty and impersonality of blind necessity. In this case, my choices have no value. All decisions are equal: the sinister actions of a drug dealer and the heroic deeds of a benefactor are equivalent, because neither of them could have been any different from what they are. The risk is that the feeling of finality, of voiceless inevitability, of being maneuvered by something other than our self, extends to our entire life.

From a philosophical point of view, this position is perhaps defensible, but from a psychological perspective it becomes hard to sustain, to the point where it is embarrassing. In all human societies the distinction between voluntary and involuntary action is alive and active. We know, too, that from the age of three a child can discern in others the difference between the two kinds of action. In some pathologies an individual feels compelled to commit involuntary acts, as in the Foix-Chavany-Marie syndrome, in which the affected person smiles when she does not want to, and cannot smile when she does want to. The distinction between a willed and an unwilled act extends to all human activities. If I were to step on your toes involuntarily, or if I did the exact same thing *deliberately*, these acts would generate entirely different scenarios (we shall come back to these issues in the final chapter).

Freedom of choice is a crucial issue in all circumstances of our life—except perhaps sleep. What value can compulsory relationships, forced learning, obligatory holidays, or entertainment have? How would you feel if a friend told you she was spending time with you out of obligation, that she came to dinner at your place out of a sense of duty? And how would you feel if your spouse one day told you he had married you because he felt obliged?

At this point it is worth summarizing some recent studies on how belief in free will can influence us in surprising ways. Note my words: we are talking here about *belief*—not fact.

In one experiment the subjects were divided into two groups. The first group read a passage from Francis Crick (the discoverer of DNA):

"You," your joys and your sorrows, your memories and your ambitions, your sense of personal identity and free will, are in fact no more than the behavior of a vast assembly of nerve cells and their associated molecules. Who you are is nothing but a pack of neurons. . . . Although we appear to have free will, in fact, our choices have already been predetermined for us and we cannot change that.

This is a frank deterministic position—it denies freedom of the will. The second group read a more neutral passage from the same book. Afterward, all subjects had to solve a series of arithmetic problems in a computer quiz. They then had to count for themselves the number of problems they had solved. For each one, they were to receive one dollar. Thus, the experimenters had deliberately given the subjects the opportunity to cheat. The finding was that those who had been primed by reading the deterministic passage cheated more than the others.

In an analogous experiment, the "determinist" subjects turned out to be less inclined to help someone in difficulty. But the most curious study was the one in which the subjects (still in two groups) had to prepare a meal for another person, and were given the choice of whether or not to add to their dish a very spicy sauce—one that makes you jump up and urgently reach for a glass of water. The determinists chose the spicy sauce—an indication, according to the researchers, of a higher degree of aggressiveness.

In yet another study, which looked at unemployed people seeking work, the subjects were given a series of questionnaires, including one on the free will–determinism continuum, in order to verify their beliefs in this matter, and also their self-image.

Afterward the researchers measured the quality of their work performance. They found that the more people believed in free will, the better was their work performance.

Finally, those who believe in free will are more capable of processing negative emotions. We know that unpleasant emotions, such as a sense of guilt, sadness, anguish, in the best case can make us reflect, and help us adapt our behavior to future predicaments. For instance, if you do not study, and you do poorly on an exam, you are disappointed, so next time you study harder. If a relationship goes sour because of your stubbornness, you feel sorry, so later you become more tolerant. The capacity to process experiences is basic to our growth. And it has been shown that this capacity is greater in people who believe in the existence of free will, while it is dramatically lower in those who do not.

From these studies we obtain the description of a full-blown typology: a convinced upholder of free will is a better worker, more honest and cooperative, less aggressive, and better able to reflect and to learn from her mistakes. In short, you will be happier with a libertarian than with a determinist neighbor. This finding of course tells us nothing about whether or not free will *exists or if the idea of free will makes any sense at all.* It simply shows that the belief in being able to exercise free choice, and feel ourselves a free agent, profoundly influences what we are.

Beliefs count. And illusory beliefs may count just as much. And implicit beliefs also matter. Often in my psychotherapy work I meet people who feel imprisoned: this is by far the most common metaphor. So I ask them to visualize their prison; they see it as a cage, of bigger or smaller size, more or less distressing. But the remarkable aspect of this visualization is that in *almost every case* the door is easily opened. The whole time, all they had to do was turn the handle! This is a truly curious fact. These people believe they are in a prison, but deep down they know they are free. Freedom, however, exposes them to the risks and responsibilities they shirk.

The freer we are, the stronger we feel. We have what is called "self-efficacy," that is, the belief in being able to influence the course of events, in being a *cause*. The more we are subjected to the will of others, or to the action of outer causes, the weaker we feel. So we may want to ask ourselves, how can we make ourselves free, or how much freer can we be? The simplest answer is to get up and do what makes you feel freer. For Ines, as we saw, it was to leave her oppressive family and go to the love of her life. For all of us, freedom is to be found in a thousand daily acts. We attain it every day, and every bit counts. Each free choice is not exhausted at the moment of decision, but lives inside us as an acquired strength.

But there is a subtler, inner way of finding freedom, and this consists in finding an inner state in which we feel free. The search for freedom is, in fact, not just a task that is manifest in the concrete world. It also involves seeking a *way of being* in which we no longer feel oppressed and obliged. Insight in this matter comes to us from the Persian poet Rumi: In his story the smart bird "dies." "Dying" here means that all our emotions, all our thoughts are temporarily reduced to zero (nothing to do with corpses and funerals). If we can do this, even for a short time, then we can return to a base from which our range of possibilities is enhanced. In electronic jargon, it is called "reset." In traditional teachings, this is meditation. In the language of this book, it is to return to one's center: the subject of the next chapter. We step back from everything inside us that is able to control, distract, or oppress us. Thus, we return to point zero. And we can fly out of the cage.

Silence

Noise makes us feel tired and confused. Silence is soothing and regenerating. It allows us to slow down or reset the activity of body, mind, and emotions: physical relaxation, emotional serenity, mental stillness. This may seem difficult, but even a moment's silence may be enough to yield good results. Imagined silence, as in this exercise, may be beneficial and revealing.

In silence we can find ourselves. And thus our will can be free.

Exercise

After several deep breaths, with your eyes closed, imagine you are surrounded by a mountain landscape. The air is clear and invigorating, the sky is blue, nature all around you is in flower. Near the top of the mountain you see a building of striking beauty: the temple of silence. You set off in its direction and soon realize that you must climb on rocks, using your hands. You are making some effort. You experience the sensations of touching the granite and of using your muscles. You feel the rock gives you solidity.

After a while the climb becomes easier. The temple of silence is much closer and the view much wider. But now, if you wish to continue, you must cross a stream. You go into the cool, clear, revitalizing water and let yourself be taken into an eddy. You surrender. It carries you down and, if you offer no resistance, it brings you back up. Water offers you fluidity. Finally you reach the other shore.

While you walk, the warmth of the sun dries your clothes. When you are almost there, you notice that the path grows narrower. On both sides you see vast spaces. The path continues through spectacular scenery—clouds and mists in the valleys, and in the distance, lakes, rivers, countryside, forests. This wide expanse gives you a sense of spaciousness.

Now you are facing the temple of silence. It is a splendid building, made of ancient material, which gives the impression of age-old solidity. Before entering, imagine for the time being leaving behind all your worries, shedding all your opinions and plans.

Now you enter and immerse yourself in a deep, regenerating silence. You see an area of light where the sun's rays burst in from outside. You enter this area of light. There, for a while, you listen to the silence. You receive the gift of silence.

Finally you come back out and, before opening your eyes, you look again at the surrounding landscape.

PRACTICAL HINTS

The various phases of this exercise refer to the four traditional elements: earth (rock), water (stream), air (empty space), and fire (sunlight in the temple). But if you prefer, you can limit yourself to the last part.

Visualization is a capacity that can be trained. It can activate and strengthen new cerebral pathways. Do not be discouraged if at first you have some difficulty or do not manage to visualize. With a little practice, this changes. You can learn from all the exercises, even those in which you seem to have no success.

THE CENTER

Our True Essence

The great Solomon, the wisest of kings, one day called Ashmodai, the chief of demons: "I have reached, so they say, a certain degree of wisdom. But I miss one vital element: the knowledge of illusion. If I do not comprehend its power, I will not be able to fully discern truth. Help me, Ashmodai, to understand illusion."

The chief of demons was silent for a moment, then said: "You must first hand me your ring." King Solomon's ring was the most precious and sacred of objects. On it was written the name of God. Without that ring, Solomon would lose all his powers. Solomon hesitated, then gave it to Ashmodai, so great was his desire to know. But no sooner did Ashmodai have the ring in his hand than he hurled it to the other side of the world. Now Solomon was in his power. Then Ashmodai hurled Solomon as well to a faraway place.

Thus the king found himself in an unknown country, alone and thirsty. Suddenly he had become a nobody. From that moment began a bewildering series of events. He wandered for twelve years. He found work as a cook, then became famous, thanks to his talent, then met the king's daughter, who fell in love with him. They married. But the king disapproved, and exiled *them to a desert. There Solomon miraculously managed to find water, start a plantation, and set up a business, which slowly flourished. He and his wife had three children. All seemed to be going well. But one day huge black clouds appeared on the horizon: a deluge was on its way. His wife and children were carried away by the waters, and drowned. Solomon lost consciousness and woke up much later, in chains. A foreign people had taken advantage of the deluge to invade the country and take its inhabitants as slaves.*

Years passed. Solomon succeeded in freeing himself, and once again prospered. Life went on with its ups and downs. Finally Solomon climbed aboard a ship. After a thousand adventures he was able to head back to his own land. During the journey he caught a golden fish. He opened it to cook it, and inside he found the most unlikely surprise: his own sacred ring. He placed it on his finger. At that very moment he woke up: he was still seated on his throne, his crown on his head. Amused and ironic, Ashmodai was looking at him: "All your mind-boggling adventures only took a few instants." During those moments Solomon had believed he was living through an entire lifetime, forgotten who he was, and lost all his powers. Without knowing it, he had been sitting the whole time on his throne.

Thus Solomon came to know the power and deceit of illusion. Thus he understood the beauty and strength of truth.

—JEWISH TRADITION

Solomon's story is the story of us all. Similar tales are found in various traditions: they show how we let ourselves be drawn in by life's affairs. Each event expands out of proportion and takes on credibility and weight until it invades our mind and becomes *all there is*—the defining mark of magic spells. Lost in the phantasmagoria of events, fascinated, terrified, defeated, or exhilarated by the turns of the story, we end up forgetting who we really are. In this chapter we will see how we can *find again our selves*—our true essence, unbound from any outer event or passing mood.

But first let us look at how we are apt to *lose* ourselves. For example, I am late to catch the plane. The car driving me to the airport is blocked in traffic. Seized by anxiety, I chide myself for not having left earlier, wonder if I will miss the plane and if I will be able to catch a later one, imagine all sorts of unpleasant consequences, etc. At that moment the matter of the plane takes over, as if it were my entire existence. I forget the wide scope of my reality, abilities, and plans. All that exists is my delay.

Other examples: I have a toothache, one so strong that it obliterates every other thought. Or I win the lottery. Or my son comes home from school with a black eye. Or again I get a fine for speeding, or a message from a friend I had fallen out with. It can be any event with the power to capture my attention. Emotions, thoughts, events, roles, sensations can all hypnotize us, carry us into a make-believe world, and tell us—or yell at us—that they are all there is.

The minute we fall under that spell, we lose our strength. Say we are overcome by a wave of depression. If the depression becomes our whole world at that moment, then we will be its prisoner. But we have close at hand a valuable inner remedy: distance. If we can see the depression in perspective, we will be free of it. Roberto Assagioli, the founder of psychosynthesis, enunciated this law: "We are controlled by everything with which we identify. We can master everything from which we disidentify."

"To disidentify": What does it mean? It means simply to put space between ourselves and a state of mind. This often happens spontaneously in everyday life. For instance, I receive an exorbitant bill. I worry about how I am going to pay it. Right afterward, I attend a concert, or meet a friend, or work out. When I again face the bill, it is less worrisome—not so large and threatening, after all. The concert, the friend, or the workout has helped me create a space between myself and the worry. Even though the bill is not a cent smaller, nevertheless I see it in a new way: because money is not all-important, because there is more to life than bills, and because I am different when I enjoy life.

We can learn to perform the same inner shift deliberately. Normally, the moment happening is all that is real for us at that time. Like King Solomon, it seems that our whole life is contained in that moment. But of course it is not so. For some, less important events, such as being late for the plane, this soon becomes apparent, and we think about it no further. For others it would seem different. How can we possibly say, for example, that a big disappointment, an important victory, a gain, a loss, a betrayal, the death of a dear one are not real? In one sense they surely are, and no one would dispute it. They are crucial events that have a decisive impact on our lives.

But in another sense they are not as real as they seem. In the Tibetan Buddhist tradition we are advised to look at each event as if it were a dream. In this way it loosens its hold on us. All events are temporal: everything changes, everything passes. Even when a misfortune befalls us, we can learn to find in ourselves a nucleus unharmed by that misfortune. Beyond the continuous flow of becoming, an immutable essence, firmly and reassuringly, always *is*. To it we can always return: from it we can draw safety and serenity. Several spiritual traditions speak of this nucleus. I will quote only one of them, the Bhagavad Gita, which thus describes the Self or center: "Weapons do not pierce the Self, fire does not burn it; nor do the waters drench it, nor does the wind dry it." The full experience of the Self is rare. But the relief of a looser involvement, a greater breathing space in our inner world, a sanctuary of peace in the midst of turmoil: these are discoveries we can all promptly make.

To distance ourselves from everything that dominates us, Assagioli suggested the exercise of disidentification: I have a body, but I am not my body; I have emotions, but I am not my emotions; I have desires, but I am not my desires; I have thoughts, but I am not my thoughts. And then: I am a center of pure awareness and will.

Sometimes people who hear of this exercise are perplexed: This is denying the body, instincts, and emotions! This is dissociation! They do not want to separate themselves from what is of greatest value to them. But it is not so. Rather, it is a matter of *letting go* of our hold. We release instead of tensing, we create space where we are cramped. If, for example, I observe my emotions, instead of identifying with them, I will perceive them in an entirely different light. In perspective, they will appear objectified. It is like the difference between, say, receiving a jet of ice cold water, and stepping back a few paces from where we see it as a shower: In the first case, we get the shock of sudden cold water that takes our breath away, the silvery spray wetting us all over. In that moment it is all there is. In the second case, we see that it is just a shower—no big deal.

Naming and defining generally help to establish distance. The Vedanta tradition has a story to illustrate this point. A lavish feast is held for the wedding of the prince—by invitation only. A man sneaks in uninvited, saying he is a cousin of the bride. The attendants let him in, but they are suspicious. The man eats and drinks liberally, flirts with the women, talks and sings loudly, mingles, and has a good time, sometimes dropping good taste and decency. After a while, seeing his unseemly behavior, the attendants confront him: Who are you, what is your name and surname, where do you live, what is your exact relation to the bride, etc. The man suddenly gives some excuse, and vanishes.

The story means to show how, by observing and precisely naming the contents of the psyche that have acquired too much power, we can keep them under control. How are we to treat intruders? Do we allow them to spread themselves around? If we attentively observe and define the emotions and ideas that absorb our world, we find that they vanish, or at least weaken. To give a precise name to our emotions helps us distance ourselves from them and diminishes their power over us. This is also what happens with the techniques of emotional writing: If we write down our most emotionally charged experiences, we generate a distance, and free ourselves from them. Our past traumas no longer weigh us down; we can live in the present.

One technique analogous to disidentification has been used by several neuroscientists. For example, Mario Beauregard of the University of Montreal has done a double series of experiments. To one group of men (whose brains were being observed through functional magnetic resonance) he showed short films of explicit sexual content, alternating with other, more neutral ones. Brain imaging revealed a normal state of sexual excitation during the erotic films. At a later time, Beauregard again showed the subjects new explicit films. But he asked them to observe, in a detached manner, both the films and their own reactions. This time, brain imaging showed great reduction in sexual excitation, and this difference was confirmed by the subjective experience reported by the participants. The experiment did not mean to repress or mortify sex, but simply showed that the male reaction to sexual excitation is controllable, and, therefore, in cases of sexual abuse, offenders cannot seek defense in the worn-out excuse: "I could not stop myself—this is human nature."

In the second experiment Beauregard showed to a group of women a series of heartbreakingly sad films. Here, imaging of the cerebral areas indicated an emotional reaction of gloom. Then Beauregard repeated the experiment, after asking the subjects to watch, in a detached manner, the films and their own reactions. This time their emotional state was greatly reduced. In other words, the subjects were able to avoid being controlled by depressive feelings. Brain imaging showed which parts of the brain were active: in the first experiment they were mainly older areas of the brain, such as the amygdala; in the second, they were the more recently evolved areas—those of the prefrontal cortex.

The goal of both these experiments was to show that it is possible to distance ourselves from the contents of our own psyche, and that this distance promotes control. Thus, we do not have to be at the mercy of emotions and impulses but can learn to master our psyche instead of being its victim. In a few moments the subjects of the experiments had covered millions of years of evolution! And this is the very same choice open to every one of us. Dante had already said it: "You were not made to live as brutes, but to follow virtue and knowledge."

Here is another contribution from neuroscience: Daniel Siegel, of the School of Medicine at the University of California–Los Angeles, coined the word *mindsight*: the capacity to watch one's own emotions and thoughts, and therefore to reflect on one's own experiences. Siegel believes the capacity for mindsight is based on a threefold disposition: openness—looking at the inner world as it is, not as we would like it to be; observation—

perceiving mental and emotional events in a broader context, detaching ourselves from automatic and habitual reactions; and objectivity—understanding that mental processes are fleeting, and that they do not constitute our identity. Siegel says that mindsight shifts the center of brain activity from the limbic area, which we share with all mammals, to the prefrontal cortex, which is an outcome of our more recent evolutionary development. To this area belong our understanding of time, the sense of identity, moral orientation, and the capacity for reflection. The central part of this area is of particular importance, because it communicates with all the others, and so has an integrative function. It is the home of mindsight.

Jeffrey Schwartz of UCLA also uses inner detachment as a means for healing. Schwartz adopts a sequence of four points to guide subjects in mastering an impulse, a thought, or an unwanted and debilitating emotion. He begins with the experimental premise that to give an emotional state a name helps us diminish its power over us. The four stages are (1) *Relabel*: Become aware of emotions, thoughts, and impulses you wish to master, and define them. (2) *Reframe*: The subject is invited to comment on a specific content. "This is not me, it is my brain." For example, if the patient has a wave of panic, he first says to himself "anxiety" or "panic," and then says something like, "It is the brain that is causing this wave of panic, but I am not my brain." (3) *Refocus*: He shifts the attention in other directions—does physical exercise or a crossword puzzle, reads a book, writes in his diary, etc. (4) *Revalue*: The last stage consists in a new assessment of the situation, also using a dialogue with the *wise advocate*, an imaginary character who represents the wisest part of us and helps us see our condition in a wider context. Schwartz started out working with obsessive-compulsive patients, but extended his method to various pathologies. Both Schwartz and Siegel adopted the attitude of detached observation (equivalent to disidentification) from the Buddhist practice of vipassana meditation.

Let us try now to understand in more detail what it means to disidentify from our various functions—starting with the body. Say our body is in some way weakened—from an illness, a handicap, or simply because of aging, or even just from fatigue or a mosquito bite. The more I identify with the sick, weak, or somehow suffering body, the more *I* am sick, weak, or suffering. But when I realize that *I am not* that process, that I can observe it with detachment, many other possibilities of well-being, growth, work, and relationships open up for me. I find more space for being other than a body in discomfort.

Identification with emotions—for many, this is the strongest one. Suppose I am overcome by fear. If I identify with fear, that becomes my world, it is my life at that moment. If I disidentify, I recognize that I *do not belong to* the fear; that I am an unchanging self, which is not overwhelmed by that or any other emotion. I realize that I am *not defined* by the momentary emotion.

Our impulses and desires are often intense and insistent. Sometimes they tyrannize us. Many spiritual traditions preach detachment. Often this has been interpreted as a negation of desire. But to suppress a desire is impossible: The desire exists and will not be defeated. The more you fight it, the stronger it gets. It is a sign of vitality. But our desires are frequently excessive, and have sway over us, as if to tell us, "You must satisfy me straightaway, it's urgent, if you don't, it'll be a disaster. . . ." Sometimes they seem to grab us by the throat: we *must* listen only to them. And we become like the *pretas*, the hungry ghosts of Buddhism, running ceaselessly this way and that, deranged and restless, always in desperate search of satisfaction in a world of imaginary objects.

We cannot suppress or eliminate desires. Yet we can certainly take our distance from them, and thus loosen their grip on us. And we also become able to distinguish between a desire (such as eating a rum-and-cream cake with blueberries) and a need (to eat).

The same goes for ideas: If I *am* my ideas, I will live with the fear that they will be shown to be false or incoherent, so I will argue against anyone who disagrees. Even if my ideas are outdated, incomplete, or contradicted by fact, I will grow fond of them and affirm them ceaselessly—since my belonging to a group, or perhaps my very existence, depends on them. To distance ourselves from our thoughts can be of great help. If we identify 100 percent with our beliefs, we risk mummifying them. What if, instead, we were to let go of our ideas and old mental habits? We could spark our imagination and widen our views.

One of the many factors that can capture us and describe who we *think* we are is our role. A role can empower us, give us a feeling of competence and respectability. To be a mother or a professor, a minister or a nurse, a soccer player or a mailman, makes us feel we have a place in society; our life has meaning, and we enjoy others' respect and consideration. This is all very well. But it is also true that roles sometimes become traps: Think of the professor who keeps being a professor even when he is at an amusement park. The mask becomes the face. The role molds us to its image—and the clay hardens so that we stay that way. A tool—the role—becomes the whole reality. Then all kinds of problems arise when we have to let go of our role: the mailman retires, the match is over, the kids grow up and leave home. We can no longer lean on the security our role previously offered us. We feel naked and worthless.

The crucial point is that when we identify with anything, it is always at the cost of something else. If we strongly identify with an idea, for instance, it excludes other ideas, and perhaps also, to some extent, our emotional and physical life, which loses relevance and meaning. If we identify with our emotions, it will be at the cost of our mental life, which will become impoverished. If we identify with a role, it will exclude all experiences unrelated to that role. A part of us will grow disproportionately strong and active, while other parts will remain underdeveloped. To succeed in disidentifying ourselves widens our vision, allows us to be more and to live more, free from the dictatorship of one single modality.

This is an ambitious project. It means going back to the part of ourselves that does not belong to time. We return to the fulcrum of our being, that part of us that always stays the same: it is the "I," which remains the same throughout our life. Through all the ups and downs of our existence, through our growth, school, work, loves, discoveries, surprises, meetings, disappointments, and dramas, there is one same "I" that is always there: the same in joy and sadness, in childhood and old age, in success and failure.

To find this nucleus of ourselves is a vital task: in it we discover our inner strength. From the center we can free ourselves of life's deceptions and chimeras and see its developments without drowning in them. This is a skill, like riding a bicycle—not easy to describe, but once we master it we can use it anytime. Examples from everyday experiences may help us understand what it is like. Imagine you are in the midst of nature, or have a day of freedom from commitments and pressures. In such moments your inner space is free. Nothing pushes, nothing oppresses you. There is no anxiety, no duty, no stress. Nothing is trying to make you do or be other than what you are. The center is like that: a space free from pressures and illusions. There, like astronauts or divers, we feel weightless and free-floating.

Normally (as we know too well) it does not feel that way. We are consumed by failure or triumph, by panic or by exaltation. There is nothing wrong with living fully and intensely through all that life brings—on the condition that we realize *it is not everything there is.*

Or imagine a cyclone coming. The sky darkens. The roaring hurricane advances relentlessly. It lifts off roofs, knocks down telephone poles and streetlights, overturns cars. A vehement wind upsets and destroys everything it crosses. Yet in the center all is calm. In the eye of the cyclone, not a breath of wind blows, the sky is clear. A great wall of surrounding cloud protects this area of quiet. The analogy applies to our life: the cyclone is storming, the eye of the cyclone is still.

To return to the center is to regenerate ourselves. Life pulls us in a thousand different directions. It disorganizes us and distracts us. How easily, especially in this age, packed with stimuli and obligations, we can lose the thread of our existence and feel torn and in pieces. Duties, worries, and demands take us away from ourselves, make us forget who we are. Though they do not touch our true being, they come with an urgency that commands our attention. By the end of the day we feel as if we have been all over the place; we feel dissatisfied and incomplete. We have run around busily. Instead of decreasing, the tasks have increased. Who can truly claim to carry out *everything*? Life is by definition messy and frayed. That is why to go back to the center means to find oneself again.

At the center it is always holiday. We can think of this in spatial terms. There are six main directions: up and down, left and right, forward and backward. Each direction is an outward movement—toward that which is other than me. According to an ancient symbolism, each movement represents one day of the week. The seventh day is the day of rest: Sunday. Quietness is at the center of all directions. It means, instead of darting here and there, just to be. After six days of work, the seventh is a holiday.

For this reason the center is, by definition, the universal remedy. Problems cannot be solved upon the same plane as that on which they were generated. If we try to solve a problem while we are stuck in it, the tangle thickens. Yet we can learn to see it from another level. Then it will be less pressing. And we will not be part of the problem anymore, but will see it from the outside and perhaps be able to solve it. However, the essential point is that the problem *has changed its status*: it is no more a basic ingredient of our identity.

The center is also the main remedy for stress. We can deal with stress in two ways. The first is to improve the situation, so to speak, from the inside. If I am tense, I can learn to relax, if I am short of breath, I learn to breathe deeply. If my thoughts are distressing, I can learn to replace them with pleasant ones. These are useful, sometimes priceless, methods. It is also possible to confront stress another way, however: that is, to detach from it, and see that *we are not* that stress. We go to a different part of ourselves, where peace reigns. That tense body is not me. Those upsetting emotions are not me. That relentless series of clashing roles and duties is not me.

A study by David Almeida of Pennsylvania State University is relevant to the topic of disidentification. Within the context of the MIDUS study (Midlife in the United States), two thousand people were monitored with repeated and detailed questionnaires that asked precisely what had happened in their lives during the previous twenty-four hours, how they had reacted, what their productivity and state of health had been, and so forth. Samples of their saliva were taken and measured for levels of cortisol, the stress hormone. Almeida concluded that by simply observing how they handled tough situations, it would be possible to predict their condition of health in ten years' time. He distinguished the "Velcro types" and the "Teflon types." When encountering a stressful event—such as being stuck in traffic or arguing with a neighbor—Velcros keep thinking about it long afterward, turn it over in their mind, and brood. Teflons instead let the event roll off them and do not give it another thought—a kind of inner fluidity, just like disidentification. Instead of clinging to difficulties, they let them slide away.

The center is silent. In the psychosynthesis exercise of the temple of silence, you visualize a temple filled with timeless silence: You enter, and let it suffuse and regenerate you. To return to the center is like going into a sanctuary. A sanctuary is a protected place: for example, a bird species can live, reproduce, and nest in it without danger. The center is a sanctuary for us: the part of us to which we can always return. It shields us—all we have to do is remember it. There we find relief. There we can regenerate. The struggles and uproars of daily living are far away and cannot touch us.

Take, for instance, Daria, who set up an organic foods farm. She bravely started the enterprise on her own, studying and collecting information as she got the business under way. She is passionate about what she does, and skillful at handling the day-to-day affairs. Yet at times she gets tired and worried. It seems she never has enough time to do everything. Every day brings new complications and unforeseen issues. One day the sprouts aren't sprouting, another the irrigation system isn't working, another it's bureaucratic problems, another it's drought, and then there are difficulties with the garbage, and so forth. She feels, as we all do at times, unable to keep up with all there is to do. It is the wearisome sensation of chronic non-completion. So she decides to waste time instead of gaining it. Each day she devotes a short period simply to *being*, to sitting somewhere and not doing anything. One evening she sits on an upturned old bucket near the bean plants. To do nothing. Evening comes, she listens to the crickets' song. She is filled with joy. She understands that to find time she has to learn to waste it. On that upturned bucket she finds her center.

Often in our lives we feel we have to *prove something*. Expectations (our own and other people's) restrain us. Our duties call us. Fantasies and ambitions entice us. Other people need us. And we must rise to every occasion. It is a deeply rooted feeling that accompanies us all our life and that we normally take for granted. This is why it is a great relief, when we find our center, to realize we have nothing to prove. This does not mean being irresponsible. Rather, it means we identify then and there with the pure part of our being, not bound by any duty or expectation.

In order to better understand these ideas, let us go to an ancient analogy. Imagine you find yourself, early one morning, on a Mediterranean beach. The sea is calm, the sky is blue. You go in the water and see the marvels of the sea: fish, shells, rippled sand . . . when suddenly a large, dark, shapeless mass catches your attention. It is lying motionless on the seabed. Somehow you manage to drag it to shore, and notice it is covered with detritus: slime, incrustations, seaweed, and shells have been deposited over the centuries, leaving a monstrous, hardened conglomerate. But you are able to remove this stuff, and you find underneath a beautiful statue of a sea god, in white marble, fashioned by a most talented hand. What looked like a formless heap was hiding a masterpiece of timeless beauty.

This thought experiment was adopted twenty-five centuries ago by Plato to elucidate the soul: under the casing of thoughts, memories, anxieties, pain, anger, and desires there lies, uncorrupted and beautiful, our soul, our true, forgotten essence. Plato believed that the soul is like the statue of the divine Glaucus. It is a wondrous statue of white marble, found at the bottom of the sea, where, coated through the centuries with sediment, it came to look like a monster, whereas it was really a god. This is the nature of our soul, our true self: forgotten in the depths of our unconscious, covered by frustrations, memories, fearful images, childhood traumas. Thus, it is impotent. We, too, can recover the statue, clean it, and give it back its original beauty.

This is the greatest catharsis. When we return to the center, we are once again in touch with the ageless part of us: without ties, without memory. It is that which is neither man nor woman, old nor young, rich nor poor.

What a relief: this is at last our true self.

Being

The basis of this exercise is impartial observation: You watch what *is* and let it flow past you, without stopping it, without interference or judgment. It is like watching a river flowing by.

You will find some short phrases to say to yourself. These are not meant to be auto-suggestion, but guides to paying attention. Beware of mechanical repetition. To facilitate contact with the inner world, keep your eyes closed.

In this exercise you place in brackets what usually holds your attention. You bracket everything that has to do with becoming—sensations, emotions, thoughts, etc. That is, you put it aside for a little while. Only by doing so can you find *being*. *Becoming* has form and movement. *Being* is formless and still.

The words "I am not my body," "I am not my emotions," etc., aren't a rejection, but a hypothesis. You take a look at what happens if you reset everything with which you normally identify. You see what is left: your "I"—the center.

It is like certain mathematical theorems in which you change a postulate and end up finding out something you did not know before. Here you start by neutralizing some old mental habits that you usually take for granted.

The last phase of the exercise may take a few seconds or perhaps just a minute.

The experience of being is ineffable.

Exercise

"I have a body, but I am not my body."

You observe the various physical sensations of the moment: contact with the chair, breath, muscular tensions, the feeling of clothing on the skin, etc. You note those sensations, but realize that you are not those sensations.

"I have emotions, but I am not my emotions."

You observe the various emotions recurring in your life, whether positive or negative: sadness and cheerfulness; anxiety and calm; anger, disappointment, hope, and so on. Because you can observe them, you are not the same as them. Emotions flow, you remain the same.

"I have desires, but I am not my desires."

You take a mental inventory of your most usual and frequent desires. Some are more intense, others less so; some are more continuous and habitual, others occasional.

"I have thoughts, but I am not my thoughts."

You look at the beliefs with which you identify most, and the ideas that most often recur in your mind. You see them all as external to yourself. Thoughts, like emotions and other contents, are, so to speak, "out there," not "in here."

"I have roles, but I am not my roles."

What are your main roles in the theater of life? However important they may be, no one role is what you truly are. Roles can change or cease; your "I" remains.

"I am."

Once you have detached from the various contents, all that is left is your "I," or self. You cannot observe it, but only be it: consciousness becoming conscious of itself.

PRACTICAL HINTS

As this exercise touches deeply rooted mental habits and beliefs, it can cause opposing reactions: "I don't agree!" "This is absurd!" In that case: "I am not my reactions."

The paradox of this exercise is that you come back to what you already are and always have been. It is like looking everywhere for a hat that you are already wearing. The "I" is the part of you that is the same as it was ten hours ago or ten years ago: the continuity and unity of your being.

This exercise is useful even if you just simply start to wonder, Who am I?

WILL

To Live Is to Choose

After walking a long time on an icy winter's day, a wayfarer was exhausted. By dusk he was in the middle of a forest, and had to find a place where he could eat and keep warm for the night. Presently, among the trees, he came upon a pleasant, well-constructed house. In the front yard an old man was chopping wood. The wayfarer asked to stay for the night. "I am not the master of the house," answered the old man, "you must ask my father, who is in the kitchen preparing dinner." He entered, and felt a pleasant warmth inside. In the kitchen was a very elderly man. The traveler asked him if he would put him up for the night. "Do not ask me," came the reply, "ask my father. Go into the living room: you will find him sitting at the table." The wayfarer grew impatient. Still, he found a decrepit old man there, drinking tea. This must be my man, he thought. But no! This was not the master of the house, either; he mumbled that the man had to ask his father, who was sitting in an armchair, smoking a pipe.

The wayfarer felt disconcerted and unnerved, and was on the verge of giving up. He became suspicious, too: They are making fun of me, he thought. This is a farce. Nevertheless, he decided to keep trying. The old man in the armchair was indeed *decrepit. From his toothless mouth came a weak voice mixed with a cough: "I am not the master of the house. You must ask my father, who is always in bed." The wayfarer could not bear it anymore. He was furious and was tempted to leave, but decided to persevere. He found the man in bed: he was so old he seemed a corpse, so weak he could not get out of bed. And he could hardly hear. He was skin and bones: only his eyes were large. In a thin voice, he said: "Go . . . to . . . my . . . father . . . in . . . the . . . crib." The traveler could scarcely hear the words. Night had fallen. He was now afraid and did not know what to do. At last, in the faintest of lights, he managed to find the crib, and there he saw a tiny but very old baby. How could this weird, ancient newborn be master of the house? In fact, he was not. He told the wayfarer to go and look inside a horn that was hanging on the wall. This was getting very eerie.*

Everything now appeared incomprehensible to the wayfarer. It was as though he were under a spell; as if there were no escape. He felt he was in the middle of an enigma. In the semi-darkness he found the horn. Inside it he could just make out a bit of ash in the shape of a face. Full of disbelief, he looked at it, not knowing if it was human. "Are you the master of this house?"—a strange question to put to a bit of ash—"May I stay here tonight?"

"Yes," came the reply, so feeble that he heard it more with his mind than with his ear, yet strong and definite: "I am the master of this house. You are welcome here." Just then invisible servants brought a lavish dinner, and candles to light it up. The wayfarer ate heartily and, satisfied, slept comfortably and warmly the long night through.

—NORWEGIAN STORY

This is an example of the will at work. It chooses a goal and reaches it. Sometimes it goes through a whole range of emotions—rage, bewilderment, fear, dismay—yet without yielding to their influence. It may find hurdles, puzzles, traps, blind alleys. It may feel like giving up. But it perseveres. This means to struggle, and to persist in the face of difficulties; and to go through to the end. Will is at the core of inner strength. In my work as a psychotherapist I see people activating their will—and I see the results: "It raises my energy level!" "It's like having a cup of coffee." "It makes a complete difference."

Perhaps we can better understand the will if we think of its absence: a feeling of impotence and indecisiveness, the ground on which depression can run rife; a state of apathy and inertia that lets other people or the events of life decide for us; conformism—following public opinion, fashion, or the party; hedonism—seeking momentary satisfaction without any further aim; shyness and fear, which stop us from openly expressing our point of view or taking a risk; shallowness, which does not allow us to deepen a relationship or enterprise; feebleness, which makes us spare ourselves, taking care not to graze a knee, not to sweat too much, while letting others bear the brunt; disorientation—the feeling of just being lost. To lack will is like trying to swim while you are carried away by the current, thrashing about desperately and being swept away because you do not have the strength to stay afloat in rough seas.

The will is an essential survival tool. It could be taught as early as elementary school, so that children become men and women who are able to be autonomous, in control of their own lives, and confident enough to leave a mark. Here we will tackle the will in its most concrete and practical aspects. When activated, it strengthens and regenerates us. "Will defines me," says Sabina, a woman who has worked on the will to move out of a long period of inertia. She decided to develop her will—and so tidied and organized her home, where old magazines and countless objects were stacked up to the ceiling; looked after her health; reconnected with her sons, from whom she had grown estranged. She felt reborn.

"It defines me" is an apt expression, since the minute we perform an act of will, we are brought back to ourselves, to that which we can and cannot do and be. The will lets us see our limits and our possibilities. It is an objective, pitiless, immediate gauge of our inner strength. Our identity is made of our single acts of will—or of their absence. A thought beckons us to run after it, a desire carries us away, an emotion may overwhelm us, mental images entertain or terrify us. A clean act of will with no fuss will bring us back to ourselves.

The will is an affirmation of oneself. It may take countless shapes: to find work, to take a bold step toward a new relationship, to ask for a loan, to introduce ourselves to someone who can help us, to travel alone to an unfamiliar country, to report an injustice, to propose and organize cultural activities, and so on. Easy? Difficult? Everything is relative: For some people, a trip of a few miles is like going to the moon. For others, requesting a loan of several million is like a walk in the park.

Self-affirmation means creating a space for ourselves, and it often involves having to deal with our own inertia or shyness, and others possibly reacting unfavorably. Indeed, when we affirm ourselves, we can expect repercussions: surprise, envy, even fear. Our affirmation is often uncomfortable for others, since it draws on limited and sought-after resources: attention, space, time, money, energy. Because we may encounter hurdles or confrontations, the shiest ones will give up. They will try to go unnoticed and avoid trouble. But in any undertaking and for any kind of expression, the necessary first step is precisely self-affirmation.

The opposite of the will is fatalism: renouncing initiatives and conceiving that the cause of all that happens to us is outside ourselves. This attitude may have some advantages, but it is ultimately harmful: people who see the cause of their destiny in the external world, who feel their lives as organized by factors beyond their control, have a greater probability of being stressed, anxious, and depressed.

If you look around, you see signs everywhere. Some of us blame fortune, get angry with others, complain about society, or, wishing our luck would change, place our hope in lotteries, inheritance, or propitious encounters. That way we do not take responsibility. If the outcome is not as we desire, we grumble. We complain about unfairness, about an adverse destiny, about how disagreeable others are; we curse our lack of time or money;

we accuse husbands, wives, kids, in-laws, bad digestion, taxes, or a slippery floor—it is always someone else's fault. The end result is self-pity, sulking, and passivity. In this case the locus of control, as psychologists call it, is external: all that happens to us originates beyond our boundaries, and we are powerless to do anything. The will implies bringing the locus of control at least partly back *inside* ourselves.

I see the passive attitude, too, in some young people (and in many others not at all) who, after a long course of study, face the working world with an expectation that heaven will shower upon them a wealth of opportunities. But most of the time life does not work that way. Sooner or later they, and we (young and old), find that even for a minimum of accomplishment we have to be proactive, meet lots of people, be interested and informed, take initiative, be on the Web, go to meetings, join societies, humbly accept apprenticeships and volunteer work, learn foreign languages, improve and update our skills, travel, and be ready to face uncertainties and discomforts. This is self-affirmation, and this is how to get ahead.

Of course, I am not praising competitiveness or activism at all costs. Choices vary immensely for each one of us. I will not push anybody's specific choice this way or that. I am just interested in how a decision—or a non-decision—happens: is fear, resignation, or distorted judgment part of the picture? That is what we should look at first.

We may decide to get cracking and activate the will. But soon we may be distracted and lose our way. Our new year's resolutions soon become worthless. New ways of life do not take hold. Efforts fail. Or we act destructively: *Video meliora proboque*, goes the Latin saying, *deteriora sequor*: "I see what is best and I approve it, then do the worst." I see all that can do me good, like a canon of rightness and perfection, like a promised land, like a vision of harmony and happiness. But then I take a more comfortable road. I am aware of what harms me and what does me good. I know I should not smoke, should consume less alcohol, eat fewer sweets, sleep eight hours a night, be kind to everybody, exercise five times a week, eat lots of blueberries, and use dental floss every day. Yet I rebel or forget or pretend to forget. Or earnestly decide to start over, yes. But from tomorrow.

Our attempts to strengthen the will often come in conflict with another part of ourselves: a dark, pleasure-loving, arrogant, irrational double who likes to take the path of least resistance and sometimes holds irresistible sway over us. Often this rebellious, naughty side of us is more attractive, whereas its counterpart is just boring and unpleasant: Who on earth wants to be on the side of Jiminy Cricket? At the end we give in and feel guilty, or think we have failed yet again. And perhaps we draw the conclusion that there is no such thing as the will. Many worthy people have reached the same verdict through a variety of respectable paths: philosophers, psychologists, neuroscientists, artists, gurus.

It is indeed an idea that, at the theoretical level, may seem elegant and convincing. But if we transpose it to practical reality, we find ourselves in trouble, because without the will, without someone in command, we are lost. We are like the *stultifera navis* of the Middle Ages: the ship of fools that goes here and there at random, roaming forever without a goal. Our life is then governed by chance: by the thousand stimuli that reach us, the people we meet, the last opinion we heard, the random events of life—forces that lie outside our power. We are, in short, the last to know what is happening to us.

Luckily we can strengthen the will. But we have to be humble. Trying to activate the will, especially if it is undeveloped, can cause a rebound reaction, and in turn more failures. Be a tough sergeant major, and you are bound for catastrophe. Become a clever, compassionate director, and the orchestra will be in tune.

When Roberto Assagioli wrote his book *The Act of Will* in the '70s, he brought to light a paradoxical situation: the will, the central faculty of our psyche, was the Cinderella of psychology. No one was talking about it. Now this situation has radically changed. Scientific studies on the subject abound, as do more accessible publications, such as the excellent book by Roy Baumeister and John Tierney, *Willpower*. In different contexts the will has been given other names, such as "executive function" (in neuroscience), or resilience, or self-efficacy, or self-regulation, or inner locus of control. But it is still about the will, albeit in one of its more specific aspects.

For the will to feel clear and effortless it has to come from the center of our being, from the self. Often this does not happen. The will may combine with various emotions, may fight against conflicting impulses, may mix with conditioned reactions. In other words, it may be a mixed bag. The great discovery here is finding the will in its pure state: sharp and sound. Picture a waiter who has to carry five cups of coffee on a tray and make his way through a crowd of people in a hurry, bumping here and there: what hope is there for the cups? Or think of a driver with passengers who are petulant and bossy, and trying to influence him at all times: who is in charge? The weak will is like that waiter or driver—pushed this way and that, or intimidated, or at best distracted. It is at risk. To discover what is our true will, we must first be in contact with our center (as described in the previous chapter). The will from the center sheds all the unpleasant connotations of coercion, phoniness, or superego with which it is usually associated. It is so much easier—and lighter.

One day Assagioli asked me, to which part of an automobile does the will correspond? The motor! I answered without too much thought. No. The steering wheel! The will is not just another force. It is a principle that directs the other forces from the outside. It is not an element that must struggle with ambition and inertia, fear and anger, euphoria or depression, while mingling with them; it is not a soccer player who runs, jumps, falls, kicks, sweats, scores a goal, or incurs a penalty; the will is more like the coach, who directs the game from the bench.

The authentic will, stemming from our center, has much more authority and vigor. One of the most therapeutic and enlightening initiatives we can take is to test the will in its purest aspect, devoid of other components. We can perform single acts of will. The studies on this topic are in agreement over this: it is possible to train the will. In fact, just as in physical training, if you overdo it, you may feel depleted afterward. But the essential point still stands: the will can be cultivated bit by bit. And when it is strengthened in one sector of our life, the effect carries over to other areas, as the Australian psychologists Megan Oaten and Ken Cheng have found. When they asked a number of people to perform small acts of will, such as refusing a piece of cake or doing some physical exercise, their subjects increased their ability to concentrate and solve a hard problem amid distractions. In other words, developing the will in one specific area automatically *transfers* to other areas of our life. Not bad for a fringe benefit.

We often think of the will as an *act* of will—a visible, concrete behavior, something we do, such as getting up earlier in the morning or taking the stairs instead of the elevator. But the act of will can also be an inhibition, a choice *not* to do. To abstain. What we choose not to do defines us and shapes our life just as much as what we choose to do: the habits we do not cultivate, the people we do not hang out with, the impulses we manage to halt, the movies we do not watch, the places we do not visit. Often an act of will involves getting rid of superfluous stuff or activities. Sometimes the decision to simplify our life is profoundly therapeutic. Elimination is illumination.

The capacity to stop an impulse can save us. It can free us from an addiction or other harmful habit. Saying no to someone (when it is perhaps easier to say yes) can be a useful and beneficial act of will. People around us make demands on us. At times these requests trespass on our space and take us away from what we would really like to do. So why do we go along? Because if we refuse, we feel guilty. How can we say no to someone who wants our company? It is the best recipe for becoming unpopular fast. How can we deny help to a friend who is floundering amid tough circumstances? And where do we find the strength to say no to someone who treats us with the duress of a tyrant?

Saying no or yes is a dilemma we face every day. It is not for me to say which is the right decision: we cannot go into the countless choices each of us faces day by day. But a yes will have meaning only if we also would have been able to say no. If it is merely consent out of fear or tiredness or feelings of guilt, what possible value can yes have?

"No" represents our identity more than "yes." A "yes" is to go with the flow. "No" is to go against the current: it stems from a later evolutionary stage, because it expresses a drive to differentiate ourselves from the environment. We have all seen a little child when she starts saying "no," usually before two years of age. Up to that time she was able only to agree. To say "no" for her equals discovering and affirming her identity: it is a turning point. But often the child who says "no" becomes more difficult; her new strength is not always acknowledged. Thus, a crucial passage is lost, and the child discovering this faculty has no encouragement to cultivate it.

To abstain from doing, in the sense of being passive, can become a conquest and a benefit. For many of us life is continual movement, an experience of doing, doing, doing—without ever stopping. We are busy and scattered. In this case, to learn to stop is what makes us grow the most. In our society, an active life is greatly emphasized, to the disadvantage of one that is contemplative, and is often regarded with suspicion and annoyance, as an excuse for lack of accomplishment. Yet for many of us, nothing could be more useful than stopping and not doing anything. Consider the idea of making room for a more contemplative rhythm, such as going for a walk or reading a book. Or what about listening to music instead of using music as a background to our frenetic activities? This is an inner strength. It is a strength that may not be seen from the outside—but in the inner world increases our well-being and the faith we have in ourselves.

We come now to the practical steps. Throughout all our lives, if we look with attention, we can find an *invitation to the will*. The call comes sometimes from a weaker, more painful, invisible, and oppressed area of our existence; at other times, from a badly organized and chaotic one. The rest of our life may be going well, but that part is a mess: for example, a difficult relationship; work that is proceeding sluggishly and haphazardly; a worrisome state of health; an interrupted project; a stagnant situation; and so forth. It is as if life were asking us to bring out our will, because difficulties are not being resolved by themselves. We need to make a choice, to be disciplined. A bit of will would make miracles, or at least could improve circumstances. At other times (often) it is not a question of using the will in a direct way. For instance, in a relationship that is not working, it is not a matter of trying to prevail over the other, but of fostering the capacity to listen. Or, if study is faring poorly, it may not be the case of pumping yet more effort and toil, but rather of changing work habits—or even courses, or the school. This invitation to the will is often hidden and enigmatic, yet it is there. If we wish to work effectively on the will, the first step is to recognize it.

The next move is more concrete. We have to work it out in practice. It is a matter of exercising the will in common situations. At the end of this chapter you will find a guide on how to apply the will to your everyday life.

And where do all these acts of will take us? Let us suppose that, using the techniques just described, you have developed the will to a certain extent. It has been an exacting task, but now you feel a strength you did not have before. What do you do with this new strength? It is like having a Ferrari in the garage. What a car! It takes on the roads like a wild beast, it roars. It is a pleasure to drive. But you still have to answer the main question: now where do I go with it?

A strong, vibrant will is useful only if we have a goal in sight. Otherwise it can even be cumbersome in its uselessness. A Palestinian story tells of a man who visits a graveyard. He sees the tombstones. One reads, "He lived eight days," another reads, "He lived one month," yet another reads, "She lived one day." "This must be a cemetery for babies," the man says to himself, but loudly enough as to be heard by a woman passing by. She says, "No, they were all grown-ups. The tombstones tell us how much each of them *really* lived."

Thus it is for each of us. Perhaps we have cultivated the

capacity to realize a project. Now we must choose which one. Or we must discover which project has chosen us. And how do we find out, how do we choose? That will happen only when we think the life we are living is worthwhile—only when we know at last what it is that makes our heart sing.

Training the Will

To train the will, you need to create an exercise that is specific to you. This means you must know the areas of your life that you feel are less strong or complete. The following exercise may help you to restore balance and stimulate efficacy.

Exercise

Using pen and paper, answer the following questions:

Of the situations in your life that are on hold, which ones would you like to resolve?
The list can be long: an unexpressed apology, an explanation not given, a promise not kept, a friendship left by the wayside, gratitude not communicated; an attic left cluttered, an unpaid debt, a borrowed book not returned; a project half-

completed, a trip never taken, a problem not solved. Our life is full of unfinished businesses. Unsettled accounts can drain our psychic energy and sometimes spoil our relations with others. When we complete a commitment we had neglected, we feel lighter.

Does it seem that others try to control your will or take advantage of you?
The most direct way to develop the will in such cases is to affirm it. When we let someone dictate the rules in our life, we become accomplices, and a dangerous habit of inequality takes hold in the relationship. Reflecting on this will bring to light any areas of your life where you could better affirm your will. The secret is to do so without anger or the wish for revenge, but in a manner that is kind and clear, and therefore stronger.

Which acts or attitudes would you like to reduce or get rid of?
Inhibition is the capacity to stop an act before it happens: we feel the urge to pass unsolicited judgment; to make an offensive wisecrack; to buy a useless item; to smoke one more cigarette. And we choose to say no. The capacity to inhibit is healthy. Contrary to repression, which is an unconscious act, it is done with awareness. At times it helps us conserve our energy. Or save our lives.

Is there any habit you would like to activate?

A habit is a series of acts that have been assimilated in such a way as to take place without special effort or attention. To activate new positive and useful habits takes time. At first this is a conscious act of will. Later it becomes a natural part of our life.

What are you afraid to do—or to be?

If you had no fear, or shyness, or terror, what would you do that you are not doing now? What initiatives would you take if you had a bit more courage—and a bit less reverential fear? This is tricky terrain. It may involve moving out of your comfort zone. Exploring it can unleash much energy.

What new initiatives would you like to start?

Everything begins with an act of will. What would you like to undertake in your life? To start a new sport, research a subject, travel, meet someone, practice meditation, write an autobiography, learn a language, reconnect with a distant relative? The longest road begins with the first step, and the first step can be merely a small one.

PRACTICAL HINTS

At this point, you have a fair amount of material in your hands. On the basis of your answers, write a list of possible acts of will that you may accomplish over the course of each day—acts that are neither too easy nor too hard; for some you may need to rub up against your own inertia, but never so much as to make you give up before starting. For example, not watching television, not eating junk food, taking care of a commitment you have long put off, making an unpleasant phone call, chewing your food properly and tasting what you eat, going to bed half an hour earlier, walking instead of driving, not reading the gossip column in the papers.

Once you have made the list, glance at it in the morning, and choose two or three acts of will for that day. Even one is enough. No exaggeration, please, or you risk indigestion. In any case, once you have embarked on this kind of idea, during the day you will find more and more chances for new acts of will. Everyday life can become a school of freedom.

PLASTICITY

The Life-Giving Power of Attention

The time had finally come: God was about to create the human soul.

It was a portentous moment. All the angels were present. It was the climax of creation: God was about to infuse the breath of life into Adam's inanimate body. In a short while Adam, from the inert matter that he was, would come alive. His heart would start to beat, his intelligence would awaken, the soul would light up his eyes. But God wanted this miraculous moment to stay secret. So He told all the angels to turn around: No one was to look. No one was to know. They had watched everything else: the creation of stars, seas, plants, and animals. The human soul was to remain a mystery.

One angel, however, decided to defy the divine injunction. His name was Eblis, and he was just too curious. He did not want to miss the birth of the human soul. He knew it would be a miracle of astonishing beauty, a wonder never to be repeated. He knew this moment contained the greatest of secrets. So when the moment came, he suddenly turned. And he looked. As he saw the mystery, his heart filled with awe. God noticed his disobedience, and grew angry. How dare this angel rebel? He decided to punish *him, and placed a mark on his forehead so all would forever be able to see. It was the mark of ignominy: this angel had disobeyed God.*

Eblis, however, never regretted his decision. He knew beforehand that God would notice his misdeed. But he was ready to endure any punishment: he was happy he had watched, because what he had been able to see was so ineffably beautiful, and the memory of it would keep nourishing him through the eons.

—MUSLIM LEGEND

The story of the rebellious angel is less about disobedience than about the prodigious act of creation. The faculty of creativity also belongs to us humans, though of course on a different scale. Any emotions, interests, thoughts, activities, or relationships we can imbue with attention, and therefore with vital energy. We can call them into being, and strengthen them if they already exist. We can also let them dwindle into insignificance.

Attention is an elementary but highly effective faculty. We all use it, often without realizing its nature and power, but rather in a haphazard, confused, or harmful fashion. Handled with intelligence, it may greatly help us in giving shape to our life, so that random events do not take over. If we make the most of this capacity, and do so consciously, our existence becomes truly *ours*, because we have discovered that what we feed and develop with our attention is our choice.

Here is an example. Suppose you decide to take up the study of the French language. You can enroll in a French course, read French books, learn about the literature and culture of the people, go to France, visit various cities, make friends with French people, refine your linguistic perceptiveness, and get to know, say, the difference between the Languedoc and the Alsatian accents. In short, you can soak up the reality of France and the French.

Thus you create a world. Suppose instead that you choose to devote time and energy to photography. In this case you get a camera, investigate the various lenses, start shooting, take a course, read the reviews of different kinds of equipment, and learn about the various types of photography: nature and landscape, portraiture, street, candid, and so on. You study the great photographers: W. Eugene Smith, Ansel Adams, and many others. And in this way, too, you create a world. This is because the acts I have described do not stand as separate entities but are infused with the vital energy of your attention; they are enlivened by it, and continue to connect and grow in you. In the case of photography, for example, you will acquire a photographic way of thinking, and, in seeing a scene or a subject, start thinking photographically, or appreciate in a new way the beauty of a landscape, or, seeing a picture in a magazine, perhaps be able to intuit what the photographer was thinking when he took it. And when you meet other photographers, you will have a common ground on which to exchange views and information. Maybe you will travel more. You will look at people and scenery with new eyes. Some photos will please you, and will be part of your positive experiences. All this did not exist before. Now it does.

We can also use this capacity to create a world against ourselves. We might see a person who looks at us with a flustered expression and think she is angry with us, but, not knowing why, we fantasize: It must be something we said or did, or it was an oversight or a blunder; so we worry, and with our attention we generate in our mind possible past and future stories, arguments, embarrassments, suspicions, even catastrophes. Then maybe we discover that the person had woken up with a headache that day, and that her bad mood had nothing to do with us. Or, again, our son went out with the car and is late coming home. We imagine all sorts of mishaps. I know quite a few parents who in this way have more than once attended imaginary funerals of their kids. Or, again, day after day we painstakingly cultivate our sense of impotence and inadequacy. With wicked pleasure and masochistic perseverance, we look for confirmation; we gather examples, seeking anything that can confirm our belief.

Look around, and you will find plenty of people who torment themselves with their worries, regrets, and resentments. They have created a world and have taken up residence in it. What has always amazed me is the common tendency to cultivate our own suffering. Why is it that we grow so fond of our harrowing worlds? Perhaps it is because the worlds we create, even when not true, are credible. Their credibility captivates us. They lead us to believe they actually exist, convince us they are the sole, definitive explanation of reality. Like ruthless tyrants, they imprison and oppress us. This happens because a series of repeated actions or thoughts creates a new brain circuit, which, once installed, tends to perpetuate itself. In any case, like a sorcerer's apprentice, we use our power to create a world. And this power often turns against us.

We are all creators, though distracted and untrained, because we do not fully appreciate the huge power of attention. In my courses I sometimes ask participants to close their eyes and revisit their childhood home. I tell them to see each room; pick up toys; and see people, touch furniture, fabrics, and objects. I ask them to smell scents and feel the atmosphere. They will usually do this exercise easily, and at the end they will say they have evoked a whole world of sensations and emotions. But the exercise is not over. Step two: I ask them to imagine being in a beautiful place they know and love, say, the site of their holidays: they will listen to the waves of the sea, or walk mountain paths, or feel the fresh air of a forest, and so on. At the end of the exercise I ask all participants, When you were back in your childhood home, how many of you thought about daily annoyances? The usual answer is, none. Then I ask, When you were in the beautiful place, how many of you thought about your childhood home? The visualization in this case, too, is so engaging that the childhood home, previously alive and present, is forgotten. We create in our mind worlds that become true and intense, but just as they have come into being, so they disappear.

Imagine you are in a large, dark room. You have a strong

torch with narrow compass, and the room is filled with all kinds of objects. You aim at random, and the torch lights up an antique table inlaid with wood and decorated with mother-of-pearl. At that moment the table exists, all the rest does not, because it is in the dark. You move the torch, so now it lights up, say, an odd, life-size plaster statue of a leopard. Now the table is gone: The statue is in the limelight. Then you move the torch again, and find a nineteenth-century cuckoo clock. Now this is the object of your attention. And so forth.

This is how our psyche works, all the time. Where do we shine the torch of our attention—onto worries, regurgitations, vendettas? On fame and gain? On impossible or destructive romances? Or on ambitions or intellectual or spiritual spheres? And, above all, with what constancy can we fuel these realities with our attention? The light gives them existence. Its absence condemns them to the dark. The same happens with actions, ideas, thoughts, feelings, tendencies, and interests. We can throw light on them, project on them our vital interest, flood them with attention. Call them into being.

The metaphor of the plant is also most fitting. When I was in second-class primary school, the teacher said: "Today, when you go home, ask for one bean. Just one. Then place it in a piece of damp cotton wool. Over the next days, watch what happens."

At first nothing happened. Every day I went to look. Then a small sprout started to come out of the bean. "Remember to add some water," said the teacher. The sprout grew. At one point little leaves began to grow. "Now put the sprout in a pot with soil.

Let it grow. Keep taking care of it." The sprout kept growing. "Give it a little pole for support." After a few weeks we put the plant in the garden, where it produced scores of other beans, the white ones with red streaks. To me it seemed a miracle.

Many years later, during my apprenticeship with Roberto Assagioli, founder of psychosynthesis, he said to me: "Attention is life-giving." Our emotions, our thoughts, are not bits of inert material. They are not mechanical events, but living processes. If we give them our attention, they grow. We can choose what we attend to. Attention, especially when consciously given, nourishes and causes anything to grow. The example of the bean came to my mind. I take an entity that is small and insignificant, that perhaps exists only as potentiality—an activity, an interest, a state of mind—and, nourishing it with attention, I cultivate it. Each of us has this power. The will directs attention. Attention carries life force.

Of course, this is true also for all that is destructive. We can focus on an obsession, and with our attention develop it. After a while it can grow out of proportion and take on a life of its own. That is why we had better be aware of our habits in directing attention. If, without realizing it, we choose toxic thoughts, they will grow, too, constellating all kinds of emotions, fantasies, and behaviors. Like the beans, they grow excessively, perhaps at great speed, and then spread and smother the other plants in the garden. If we concentrate on a fear, worry, resentment, or irritation, we end up making them gigantic. Thus, for example, I can cultivate my worry for the future: I seek confirmation in the newspapers and on television, hang around people who have the same anxiety, find everywhere—in fragments of conversation, urban settings, events from everyday life, strangers I meet on the train, facial expressions, dreams, headlines—valid reasons to be afraid. I end up seeing what I fear: And so, with great diligence, I cultivate just that which I wish to be rid of.

Many recent studies on the brain show precisely this phenomenon: I am speaking of neuroplasticity. Contrary to the previously held credo, neuroscience has for a while been championing the idea that the brain, far from being an immutable entity, is continually changing. Until a few decades ago it was a neurophysiological dogma that once the brain had developed, it remained the same for the rest of the person's life. You would see huge character changes take place in people, or the flowering of musical, mathematical or manual aptitudes, or the birth of philosophical or religious beliefs, or the acquisition of new habits. Yet you were told that the brain was unchanging. This situation could not but generate a great schism between the sciences of education and psychotherapy on the one hand, and neuroscience on the other. In real life you saw individuals making spectacular transformations. Yet neurophysiologists (as they were then called) told us everything in the brain had stayed the same.

In recent years neuroscientists have dramatically changed this postulate: The brain, they say, can be modeled and transformed. Old neuronal pathways can die and new ones can be born. It is not only actions that change the brain, but also thoughts. For example, the brain of a student is different after she has intensively studied a subject. This is an illuminating principle in psychotherapy as well as in education. In cognitive psychotherapy you train the depressed patient to interpret life events in a less catastrophic fashion; or the obsessive-compulsive patient to perceive seemingly irrepressible urges, such as frequent hand washing, in a different way, as less important, and as not really being part of his identity. Now we know that such changes in thought affect the brain as well. In a greater context, a taxi driver, a ballet dancer, a goldsmith, a flautist, and an electronic engineer have all changed their brains over the years, depending on the habitual images and thoughts they have had, and the acts they have performed day after day—corresponding to the direction of their vital energy. Some parts will be more developed than others. We have all made our brains into a specialized tool. Anatomy is destiny. But we can mold anatomy.

Neuronal geography takes a specific shape for each one of us. We all carry in our brains the individual code of our existence, and the brain is the microcosm that contains and represents our entire being. So all of us have the ability—and the responsibility—to shape our own brain. And it can all happen in a very short time. A study on computer skills and brain plasticity concluded that there are indeed specific differences between the brain of a beginner and that of a computer expert. But these differences were bridged with as little as five hours' training.

Plasticity, neuroscientists tell us, is competitive: a true struggle for survival takes place, because the available space is finite. The new nerve pathways replace the old, just as new habits supplant the old ones. William James called it "the expulsive power of positive ideas." So the moral of the story is: The best way not to worry about death is to be interested in life. If you do not want to stay at home agonizing over ill health, go for a brisk walk. Instead of complaining about loneliness, find out what you can do to meet people. And so on.

The brain we create becomes the home we inhabit. In an Asian story a king asked a builder to build him a house. "Make it really beautiful: Use the best materials. Don't mind the expense—I want a masterpiece."

The builder, in truth, was a bitter and resentful person. He was near the end of his working life, and wanted to put some money aside. He therefore hoped to earn more by cheating wherever he could. Without telling the king, he decided to use cheap materials. The beams would give way after a while; the plaster was mixed with soil; the marble was of inferior quality; the sewer was badly designed, and after a few months would start to stink. The workmanship was hurried and unskilled. And more besides. After a short time the house was ready.

And here comes the crux. The king had secretly wished to reward his subject. He had made him build the best possible house because once it was finished he wanted to surprise him by making a gift of it. "The house is yours. You may go and live in it."

Thus, the embittered builder went to live in the fraudulent home he had built with his own hands. And he dwelt for the rest of his life in the house of deception.

It is the same for us. Day by day we live in the house we construct. We live in the brain we have modeled. What materials have we used? What principles, what project? What coherence?

By now a basic element should be clear. We are dealing with two fundamentally different conceptions of our life. According to one, life just happens to me. Though I am involved in the flow, it is in a passive way. Thus, all events catch me off guard, unless they are habitual events, in which case they imprison me. I feel unable to decide. Sometimes I am overwhelmed by circumstances. Moreover, my thoughts and emotions are just what they are—inevitable. I am made this way. This conception underlines weaknesses.

The other is the creative conception: My life is my own doing. It is a result of my choices. This allows me to feel I am the author of my existence, or at least the interpreter. I give it meaning and direction. My thoughts and emotions vary, depending on my attitude toward them. This disposition generates a great deal of inner strength.

I would now like to speak about a power that is symmetrical to the giving of attention: the power of ignoring. Like paying attention, ignoring is not a neutral act, but can have important, even dramatic, consequences. Try to think—I am sure this has happened to you—of a time when someone ignored and excluded you. That person was greeting others, talking with them, laughing, joking, collaborating, but treated you as though you were invisible. He did not even look at you, spoke not a word to you, excluded you from his attentions. How did this attitude make you feel? Much depends on who the perpetrator was, but the most common reaction would be to feel miserable.

If you really want to withdraw attention from someone, you have to do it gradually and with great caution. We often underestimate the dangers of such a withdrawal. In my work I have often heard people talk of the sudden severing of ties, with no explanation given. Someone decides to exclude another from her life. Up until that day he had enjoyed friendship, warmth, maybe love, a long tradition of dialogue, common interests in work or play. Suddenly one of them disappears or somehow retreats from the other, in a surprising, peremptory, and total manner. Or, without giving any reason, she expresses the wish not to see the other anymore. The effect on the other person can be catastrophic: on his self-esteem, security, confidence, and capacity for loving. It can create an emptiness that may never be filled; a terrible, incurable nostalgia. Often the retreating person does not realize the harm she is causing. After all, it is not an active behavior—she is not delivering any insult, blow, slander, or wrong. She simply vanishes. We have the right to disappear, don't we? Perhaps, but if we are going to do so, it would be best, in my view, to do it gradually, with due explanation.

While the decision to ignore can be cruel when it concerns people, in our inner life it can be most fruitful. We can use the technique of indifference with all our traits, thoughts, and mental habits that irritate or dishearten us.

Let us imagine we are tormented by a thought: for example, an economic worry that leads us to believe everything is going to rack and ruin and we will die in the poor house. Or suppose that the fear of flying oppresses us, yet work obliges us to fly. Or consider the devastating feeling of a love affair ending badly. One possibility is to ignore the thought. And slowly it will diminish and be absorbed in darkness of oblivion.

I can already hear your objections: But you *must* think about these things! This objection is of course well taken and at least partly right. It is best to use the technique only after having weighed and evaluated the thought or emotion that haunts us or weighs us down. The point here is that we have two opposite ways of treating every thought and every emotion: soft and hard. This distinction is crucial for all of us, doubly so for psychologists, psychotherapists, and educators. The soft way is giving full credit and attention to a thought or feeling (in ourselves or others) when it emerges. The economic worry is perhaps a signal we ought to consider. Behind the fear of flying may be an old trauma or a real need for greater safety. The badly ended relationship may point to the need for a further step: seeing the other person again, clearing the air, making peace. Every emotion, every thought, every element of our psyche has something to tell us about ourselves and the world. It is wise to listen to it.

But at some point we just may want to say, Enough! This is the hard way. Just as we have given our attention, so can we withdraw it. We do not have to cultivate fear, anxiety, or anger with the care and devotion we give to a plant in the garden. We can decide to take the whole array of unpleasant emotions— worries, dread, obsessions, negative ideas, catastrophic fantasies, depressive feelings, disappointments and resentments, regrets and remorse—and treat them the tougher way: we decide *not* to give them our attention, and so not to let them grow excessively. To subtract attention from these emotions and thoughts brings an astounding result: it starves them. Each time they arise, we decide to get involved in something else more interesting. We no longer give them credit or importance. We act as if they were not there. Deprived of our attention, they tend to wither and die.

What we do not attend to does not exist—or at least it looks that way. In a famous experiment, each subject is asked to watch a film in which basketball players are quickly passing the ball to one another. The subject has to count the number of passes. It is not easy, because the game is fast moving. At one point a gorilla walks into the room (that is, a man dressed as a gorilla), and walks around, beats his chest, then leaves. But the subject is busy counting the passes, and (most of the time) does not notice the gorilla. When the experimenters show the subject the film afterward, he cannot believe the gorilla was there, and even suspects he has been deceived. Yet it is no deception: what we do not pay attention to, no matter how conspicuous, disappears. We have a choice. What do we want to cultivate, and what do we want to let wither: love or venom, infamy or loyalty, desolation or cheerfulness? The lack of attention shapes our world.

Back to the hard/soft dilemma. We would do well to find the right balance. In general it is best to start with the soft attitude, because every idea, intuition, or feeling in principle has something to tell us, even if it is illusory or disheartening. Too much attention to certain elements, however, turns us into neurotics and can set up an obnoxious kind of self-indulgence, an obsessive and pampering self-analysis. Unfortunately this is the danger of some psychotherapies that do nothing other than cultivate the very forces or processes the patient wants to be free of.

On the other hand, a hard attitude alone is fascist: One forges ahead without taking into account the signals life is so clearly and abundantly offering. This produces tension, repression, and excessive strictness with oneself. No, we cannot always pretend nothing is the matter. We have to choose the right timing and wisely gauge our attention.

Here is an example: Fosco is a forty-year-old man obsessed by memories of his childhood, deep wounds that keep hurting; as a child, day after day, he witnessed fights between his parents that often ended in violence against his mother. This repeated nightmare caused him a great deal of suffering. As soon as he closes his eyes, the scenes come to mind and he relives them: screams, threats, beatings, pain.

The best way to free oneself from traumas is to relive them till they exhaust their emotional charge. At least this is the first essential step. But this is often not sufficient, because the trauma continues to reverberate throughout the whole organism, as if it happened merely hours before. This is how it is for Fosco, who is tortured and persecuted by these memories. I ask him once more to evoke them, and he relives the worst scenes. Even though he has done this many times, his face distorts in a mask of suffering. After a while I ask him to change gear abruptly. I know of his passion for classical music. I suggest that he evoke a musical theme he likes. He is astonished at my request. How could such a thing come into my mind? I insist, and he chooses the theme of the Goldberg Variations by Bach, his favorite composer. His forehead immediately relaxes. You can almost see the theme playing in his mind. I then ask him to evoke another melody: he chooses the Sanctus of the Mass in B Minor. This time I can see, in his expression of half-surprise that he is better able to plunge into the music. Another theme: the last movement of the third Brandenburg Concerto, the one for strings only. His face continues to change, as he perceives the beauty. He has changed universes. He picks yet another theme: Mozart's Piano Concerto no. 21—the famous adagio.

Later Fosco tells me that these themes come back to him in daily life—they comfort and encourage him. But for a while he treats musical thoughts as "fantasy," and traumas as "reality." Then he realizes they were just two different wavelengths, and it is he who can decide, and can place his attention wherever he thinks best. He takes more control of his life. Whereas before he felt prisoner of a job he did not like, now he can produce new projects in the theater and at school, in fields that have always been more congenial to him.

After a while, however, Fosco returns to a state of negativity. He is angry and depressed, and during the session he lets himself go in an outburst of self-blame: "I am a fool," "I am worthless," "I will never amount to anything," and so forth. Then something unpredictable occurs during the session, one of those fortuitous events that seem to happen just at the right time. Jung called these "synchronicity." A famous example is of his patient telling him she had dreamed of a golden beetle, and right at that moment a gust of wind blew open the window and a golden beetle (a rare species in Switzerland) flew into the studio. Fosco and I had started the session during a violent storm that had blackened the sky with clouds. Then the clouds dispersed, some remaining still black, others turning golden, or white—a wonderful display. Finally, against this background, a rainbow appears, quickly intensifies, and spans the entire sky. A second rainbow appears, its colors inverted and fainter. Fosco is amazed. He contemplates the rainbow, oblivious to any comment I make, so I keep quiet. Minutes pass, the rainbow disappears. Fosco has changed visibly; he is in an altered state of consciousness. "And your troubles?" I ask him. "Where have they gone?" He has forgotten them. All he has done is shift his attention—this time with the help of the cosmos. He is now convinced. What you pay attention to is real. At the end he thanks me even for the rainbow.

To understand that our personality and our life can be molded, and that this is our responsibility, gives us back a sense of power over ourselves. We see that our life is in our hands. This is very different from a vague and boundless freedom. It is untrue to say we have unlimited possibilities. What we have, on the contrary, are weak points and limitations that have to do with time and energy, genetics and upbringing, and the present situation. If freedom were unlimited, it would lose all value. It is hard to imagine how our life would be, but most likely it would lose its meaning and beauty, too.

On the other hand, it would not be right to say we are wholly determined. Often we are controlled by conditioning, habits, and mechanisms that lie outside our consciousness. But it is also true that our future is open. Our freedom is not measured so much by its range as by its practicability.

We are not like the carefree gods. Nor are we obedient cogs in an impersonal machine. We are men and women who can, if we so choose, activate our freedom and give shape to our lives.

Creating a World

Each day we generate and feed inner realities, and we let other ones disappear. But we do so without being aware of how we do it. Here we learn to do so consciously, and to place this operation under the control of the will. It is important to understand which aspects of ourselves (however strong) we want to disempower, and which ones (however weak) we want to reinforce.

Exercise

After closing your eyes, imagine going back to your childhood home. Revisit each room, letting memories emerge; remember the smells, touch your toys, perceive the atmosphere of the place. In a few minutes you re-create a world.

Now leave your childhood home, and change scenes. You are in another place, one that gives you a sense of well-being—for instance, nature, or a friend's house. Spend some time here, too. Allow the images to become vivid. Re-create as far as possible the various visual, auditory, tactile sensations, perhaps also taste and smell.

Now return to yourself in the present. In a few minutes you have seen how it is possible to switch on one world and let another one disappear.

Now think of some aspects of yourself that you would happily do without: obsessions, fears, worries, regrets, remorse, depressive inner monologues. Write a list of them. These are inner realities that shape your days. You cannot eliminate them from one moment to the next, but you can learn to reduce their importance. Instead of feeding them, you withdraw your attention. Every time they arise, you turn your attention to something more worthwhile.

Now think of aspects of your life to which you would like

to give more strength: states of mind, activities, interests, relationships, values. Write a list.

Choose an item from your list, and think of all you can do to emphasize this reality. For example, let us say you would like to improve your health. What can you do? Learn to breathe better. Eat more nutritious food. Take walks in nature. Go to a gym. Take a tai chi course. Learn how health is also a psychological fact. Read books on the subject. Research using the Internet. Meet people with a similar interest. And so on. In this way you create a world. Then you can go and live in it.

PRACTICAL HINTS

What you have learned in this exercise you can apply to everyday life. At any moment you can decide where you want to put the accent of importance.

Wherever you place the attention, that is where your vital energy will flow.

MASTERY

The Many Benefits of Self-Regulation

A young man's wife died, and he was desperate.

He could not resign himself to this loss. He went to his wife's grave, and there, at dusk, her spirit appeared. "Do not grieve," she said. "Though I am gone to another world, I am still around."

"I want to follow you," said the husband. He simply could not accept losing her. She tried to dissuade him, but it was in vain. So she said: "During the day I disappear. But I will wear a red eagle feather on my head. You will always be able to see it. Follow the feather. Follow me to the other world."

In the soft pink light of dawn, the woman became transparent, her image ever dimmer. Then she vanished. But the husband could follow the red feather. The invisible wife moved quickly, climbed over rocks, walked on mountain paths, through forests, over streams, down steep cliffs. She was light and fast. The husband had trouble keeping up. All he saw was a red feather fluttering onward.

They traveled this way for days and days. Finally they arrived at a lake: The surface shone like a mirror. There, the wife dived in, and the husband saw the feather disappear underwater. He realized that in the depths of that lake lay the world of the dead.

He understood he could not follow his wife there. But presently some owls, who were also wise men, came to his aid and gave him directions. They would sprinkle on his face a magic liquid that put him to sleep; he would wake up at dawn in an unfamiliar place; from there he should head toward the Morning Star; this way he would find his wife. There was, however, one rule he had to remember and respect at all costs: He would have to control his impatience, and the moment he found his wife, under no circumstances was he allowed to touch her; however great the temptation might be, he would have to wait until the moment when they were both safe and sound at home.

And so it came to pass. The husband woke up. He found his wife, still asleep. Then she woke up, too. She was alive, in flesh and bone. She looked at him and said, "Your love is true and beautiful, your will has been strong. You have been brave. Only thus were you able to find me." The man was overjoyed.

They began the return journey. For several days they walked together. The man kept the warning in mind: he must not touch her. A moment came when she wanted to rest, so she lay down on the grass and fell asleep. The husband looked at her. He was happy to have found her. They had a life together before them. He knew he ought not embrace her till they were home again. But she was beautiful. He loved her. His passion was irresistible. What harm could it do if he were to caress her for but a moment?

In the end he touched her. Straightaway she woke up in tears: "You loved me very much—but not enough. You had not the patience to wait. Now all is lost." Little by little she disappeared before his eyes, till nothing remained.

Only a lone owl hooting on a faraway branch.

–ZUNI INDIAN LEGEND

Traditions from every country have stories that warn us of the dangers in lack of self-control. Pandora knew she must not touch the box, but the temptation was too great: She opened it and all kinds of horrors flew out—toil, sickness, discord, old age. Woes spread among humankind and continue to this day. Orpheus was not supposed to turn around while bringing Eurydice out of the underworld, but he yielded: his desire to see her was too great, and he turned—she remained Death's prisoner forever. For a plate of lentils, Esau gave away to Jacob the right to become Isaac's successor and lead the Hebrew people. Lot's wife, fleeing with her husband from Sodom before its destruction, disobeyed God and looked back. She was turned to stone.

Again and again the story repeats itself: how hard it is to resist temptation. We see it in fairy tales, too. The first two little pigs built their homes of straw and of sticks, as they wanted to get it done in a hurry and go and play. But the wolf blew their houses down with one breath.

To toil is tiresome. To wait is tedious. To yield is human. After all, we are not as self-possessed as we may think. We are irrational, impulsive, and incapable of controlling ourselves. The only way to get rid of a temptation, says Oscar Wilde, is to yield to it.

Or perhaps not. In a well-known experiment, a four-year-old child is left alone in a room. Before her is a sweet: she can eat it straightaway, but if instead she resists temptation for a quarter of an hour, she may have *two* sweets. One out of three children manages to wait. Unlike the impatient husband, Orpheus, Pandora, Lot's wife, Esau, and the first two little pigs, one-third of the children control themselves and adopt various strategies: they think of something else, look the other way, talk to themselves, close their eyes, sing a song, imagine the sweet is not real but painted. Each in his or her way manages to resist. If they focus on the sweet, the temptation becomes irresistible.

Ten years later these children do better at school and have more friends. Their reasoning, social skills, and academic proficiency are better than those of their peers. They are more capable of handling stress and concentrating on the task at hand.

The original experiment was done about forty years ago by Walter Mischel, and later repeated in a multitude of variations, which increasingly confirmed the immense relevance of the findings. My favorite is of a group of children, some of whom were given a Superman suit, in which they played for a while, acting the character of Superman (others were instead dressed as Mr. Dash). Afterward, when tested for their ability to postpone gratification, they showed greater self-control. Evidently the way we perceive ourselves influences our capacity for self-regulation. We also know that the ability to delay gratification is active in some animals: chimpanzees, parrots, pigeons. It is an adaptive capacity.

As time passes, longer-term data have become available to us. New Zealand researchers recently published the results of a study done over a period of thirty-two years. We also have data from the subjects of the first experiment, who are now enjoying the ups and downs of middle age. The children who were able to resist temptation, now grown up, are less likely to be obese or have problems of drug abuse. They have fewer sexually infectious diseases, better dental health (hygiene and regular checkups). Their salaries are higher, their marriages more stable. They are less likely to have done time in jail. They do more physical exercise, and even use the car seat belt more. It comes as no surprise that they live longer.

We know that delaying gratification offers many benefits. Many of us, however, struggle. In this matter a collective complicity is at work right before our eyes. Our economy is based precisely on lack of self-control. We see chocolate that is fiendishly tempting, a dress or pair of shoes, a car or the latest model smartphone, and we rush to buy it.

Yielding to impulses that can give immediate pleasure is a residue from childhood—wanting everything straightaway. Sometimes this irresistible desire comes with the more or less explicit belief of being in credit: Gratification is my *due*. Desire is transformed into right. No delay is tolerated, no frustration endured. Missing gratification generates disdainful annoyance, sometimes rage. People whose expectations are frustrated may show an expression of supercilious astonishment, as if it were absurd and unacceptable that the world did not operate according to their wishes.

This way of dealing with frustration is dangerous, because it exposes us to more disappointment than is necessary, and to easy manipulation. It places us at the mercy of the tantrum-throwing child within us, who whines, yells, and stamps his feet, totally dependent on the satisfaction of his impulses and desires. It is a handicap that causes us to miss opportunities and exposes us to all sorts of damage.

Every day we see how dangerous lack of control is. We hear of politicians and other VIPs involved in sex scandals; of futile murders committed; of fights, words, and rash acts bringing serious and long-lasting consequences; purchases made on the spur of the moment; slavery to drugs and gambling. How often have we regretted following a whim? Impulses are centrifugal: they take us away from our center toward something other than what we are. There is nothing wrong with this: our own survival is based on the capacity to be pulled out of ourselves. However, if this tendency is not balanced by a symmetrical capacity to return to ourselves—a centripetal tendency—then the result will be a chronic lack of balance: a perpetual dispersion that causes us to wander among a thousand temptations, like a traveler roaming through many lands and forgetting the way home.

The capacity for self-control, on the other hand, is the basis of our civilization. It means being able to control aggression, greed, and impatience; to predict the effects of our actions; to develop long-range projects; to cooperate with others. It is, of course, work in progress: We are still a long way from full maturity. The more we acquire skill in this domain, the greater will be our inner strength.

The main strategy is to distance ourselves from an impulse so as to render it less powerful. This is what I referred to earlier as "disidentification." The discovery that we can create space between ourselves and the contents of our psyche is a milestone. The opposite of this strategy is for us to be ruled and overpowered by our impulses and desires. They take us by surprise, assail us with vehemence, make us believe they are irresistible. They convince us they are the best option on offer. We can, however, learn to detach ourselves from their influence. It is like the difference between being shoved in the street by a passerby and watching the same scene from a high building. In the first case the violent impact takes us by surprise; it is unpleasant, and we protest against the bad manners. In the second, we are not flustered, and we see the same event in a broader context, with equanimity.

To know how to detach from an immediate impulse—that is the secret. Often this means simply to wait. Those who are capable of waiting can remove their attention from the object of desire, and nurture a plan, build it piece by piece, and proceed without immediate rewards. This is true for a course of study, in which we have to spend many years doing hard, sometimes boring work in order to complete any project, which demands that we put in effort and encounter frustration, opposition, boredom, other people's lack of understanding, and many other kinds of obstacles. The development of regular discipline is essential, and often must be without encouragement, reward, or gratification. This is the mark of true maturity: rather than give in to the first impulse, we become able to see far ahead, reflect on goals and methods, withstand the sway of emotions, reframe disappointments, and maneuver our way through a thousand obstacles. It is the capacity to place less value on a present that is tugging at us with false urgency, and more emphasis on a future that is still invisible.

For those who are unable to delay gratification, time is an enemy. They experience it as a hindrance that causes distress and stands between them and happiness. It is perceived as a source of suffering, because it separates them from pleasure. But time can also be a friend and can save us from complications, solve problems, put difficulties on hold, and minimize our dramas. A story from the North American Iroquois Indians tells of two children who were yelling and fighting. Their mother intervened: "This is the way to solve the problem. Take three twigs and make a tripod. Then place it somewhere in the forest. In one month go back, and have a look at what has happened: If it has fallen southward, one of you is right. If it has fallen northward, the other wins the argument." The two children liked the idea and went straight to work at it. After one month they remembered the tripod and went into the forest to see which way it had fallen. But in the meantime the twigs had decomposed, so there was no way of telling. And the two children could not even recall anymore why they had argued in the first place.

Time, in other words, is a healer—that is, if we give it a chance to help us detach from our impulses and learn to tame them. Often enough, if we wait a little, we will be able to reach a clear judgment. It is sometimes wiser to postpone. Assagioli used to say, "We don't solve our problems, we forget them" (well, perhaps not all of them).

And now let us turn this subject upside down. Let us imagine that we feel like *delaying* instead of anticipating. This is what happens when we put off until tomorrow what we could do today: bills to pay, difficult telephone calls, dull reading, meetings we dread, nightmarish bureaucracy, and other thankless tasks. These are all jobs we tend to postpone. This, too, is a childish attitude, because it wants all unpleasant chores to disappear as if by magic. But we know full well that these chores will stand there waiting, and will indeed grow larger and become more expensive and more threatening as time goes by. Here time is not the grand healer: the dull reading still needs to be done, the bills do not pay themselves. In the end, circumstances will oblige us to face the music.

The tendency to postpone is bad for the economy, because it is the source of countless delays and a huge waste of energy. This is why studies abound on the subject. It has been shown that individuals who are prone to postponing are less healthy, first of all because they tend to put off their medical and dental checkups, and are therefore likely to be late—perhaps too late—in dealing with health issues. But they are less healthy also because they have greater anxiety, which lowers the efficiency of their immune system: They have more colds and flu. On top of this, they have more gastrointestinal problems and suffer more from insomnia. This is understandable, since people who tend to postpone transform their future into an overcrowded storehouse of onerous tasks. Just think of a duty you have put off. How does it seem to you? Probably it will feel like a burden, which the illusory and temporary relief of postponement relieves only in part. The future is no longer a free space, but a dusty depository packed with duties and stuff that still need to be done. Is that where you want to be going?

Chores on our to-do list are not inert entities that, left undone, remain unchanged. They take up space. David Allen, author of the book *Getting Things Done*, holds that the unfinished tasks are like big files that eat up space in a computer's memory—and slow the computer down. Moreover, the sooner a task is due, the more difficult it will seem to us (as a study by Gabriela M. Jiga-Boy of Swansea University in Wales has shown). It is as if the difficult task—finishing a thesis, or filling out a complicated tax return, or tidying the attic—were pressing heavily on our life, making us breathless and compressing the time we have left for it. The more we postpone, the more dramatic the situation becomes. Here, too, time is an enemy—not because there is too much of it, but because there is too little.

The main reason we postpone is that we have no desire to do what we must. Life often gives us hard and unpleasant jobs. We prefer to have fun and take the path of least resistance. The more arduous course of getting the job done can wait. Better to go to the movies than to pay the rent, or to surf the Net than to study, or to relax than to read a complex book. We replace the reality principle with the pleasure principle. Like Pinocchio, we play truant and go to Toyland. But sooner or later we wake up with donkey ears.

The good news is that if we do the same things with an attitude of *willing*, instead of *having to*, then time passes more quickly. Usually we deal with annoying duties against our will, spurred only by the anxiety over the consequences of not getting them done. That way it feels like moving a boulder: time drags. If instead we face these tasks willingly, our attitude is going to be more purposeful and active; we will feel more in control; and time—as research has proved—will seem to flow faster. We will experience quite differently the very same job if we subjectively feel it as pressure, or if we see it as an act of will. It all depends on how we construct it inwardly.

Here, too, we see that the capacity for self-regulation touches deep levels of our psyche, given that it can even influence our perception of time. One could write volumes about our relationship with time: it is one of the great mysteries of human life. Now and then time seems to pass too slowly, and at other times too quickly; we feel as though we were inside time, having to obey its laws and rhythms, yet in certain magical moments time seems to stand still. To be sure, self-regulation by itself does not place in our hands the key to the enigma of time. But it helps us not to fall under its dictatorship, and it gives us a good start in understanding and mastering it.

Now let us take stock. The two themes of this chapter—immediate gratification and the tendency to postpone—may appear as discrete subjects, but in reality are the two sides of the same coin. We want instant gratification because we wish to avoid the effort of waiting. We put off the effort of an unpleasant or boring activity in order to have a good time *right now*. In both cases we take the path of least resistance. We prefer momentary pleasure at the cost of using the will.

By correcting and resolving these deficiencies, we develop our capacity for self-regulation. How can we do this? The answer is simple. If we want to learn to delay gratification and to stop procrastinating the tasks we want done, we do them as an act of conscious will. When a seemingly urgent request or a seductive stimulus comes (they come all the time), we can wait before we give in. After a while it is not as impelling, the object of pleasure that seemed indispensable has lost some of its interest, and chances are we can withstand the impulse. We may succeed in taking credibility away from the stimuli that bombard us. One of my sons, when he was a child, on entering a toy store would want to buy nearly everything (with his savings). So I would say, All right, but wait a while and let's see if you then still have the same wish. He would agree, and almost always the desire would fade. And he would save his money. We can do the same for our inner child, and say, Wait, think about it, weigh it up. Now, we might not wait a quarter of an hour, but perhaps a week or a month. Anyone who wants to sell us something knows this tactic too well, which is why he makes a "special offer" to be accepted within a short time—take advantage now, because it will not be there tomorrow.

The same goes for the tendency to procrastinate. We can learn to do *now* what must be done—especially if we think about the advantages. One of my clients, who every day had to reply to a great number of e-mails, tended to put off the task and do more interesting things. He was besieged by e-mails: he considered them demanding, invasive, obnoxious (understandably). I asked him to divide them into categories. He made the following: e-mails that did not strictly require an answer; e-mails that he had to answer, but only after reflecting on them and allowing time for the reply to mature; and e-mails that needed an immediate answer. He adopted this method, and devoted to e-mails a time of day when he did not need his sharpest mental powers, which he devoted instead to more important activities. We learn to stop procrastinating by small, sudden acts of will that cut through inertia and hesitation.

Indeed, activating the will is a matter of saying many times "no" or "not now," and also saying "now!" without delay or resistance. It also helps to split a task into smaller and easier segments, or to reflect that postponing will cause hindrances to not only ourselves, but others as well.

Here one might object: to delay gratification or to postpone our duties is wrong—if we take for granted that our main value is productivity. But if we have other priorities, such as relationships with people, happiness, fun, enjoyment of beauty, and so on, then to be efficient becomes less important. After all, those who do everything in the fastest time, and relentlessly go through life like a well-oiled machine, often wind up being unfulfilled. Above all, they forget the most important values: love, play, reflection, and enjoyment.

This is a legitimate objection, and allows us to see just how complex human life is, how multifaceted our nature. Control, if pursued as an end in itself, risks making us dry and obnoxious. No doubt this is a risk. You have met people who are perfectly in control of their lives: their finances, work, home, car, family—everything is in perfect working order. But the price for perfection is high. Control has become a fetish to some people, their life goal. Such super-controlling people often lack imagination, and do not enjoy life much. Do you want this to be your ideal model? Probably not. But the question here is not how do we get complete control, rather how much are we at the mercy of our impulses, of false promises of happiness at bargain prices, or else prisoners of a paralyzing inertia?

There is yet another objection: think of the state of grace, the best moments of our life—the experiences in which we feel inspired, or filled with happiness. These events, though highly desirable, seem to be outside of our direct control. Mihaly Csikszentmihalyi has studied them in depth. He calls them *flow*—an effortless, unhindered fluidity, without rigidity or excessive self-consciousness. For years he interviewed thousands of subjects, and found out what happened right when they were having these experiences: while playing the violin or reading philosophy, cooking for friends or riding a motorcycle at 150 miles per hour. Paradoxically these moments of sublime spontaneity—in which everything happens by itself and appears to transcend all control and all egocentric preoccupation—are the greatest expressions of mastery. These experiences, as described by those subjects, were in no way examples of yielding to random impulses or a state of passivity, but the result of long-cultivated self-regulation: "The best moments come when the body and mind of a person are extended to their limit, in a voluntary endeavor toward a goal that is difficult and worth the effort."

In conclusion, all the themes in this chapter point in one direction: overcoming our childishness, freeing the cluttered mess of our drives or the inertia of procrastination, seeing through the naive hope of living in an eternal state of reward with no discomfort and no effort. The art of self-regulation helps us win freedom and autonomy, and enjoy subtler and more lasting pleasures. The universal image of this state is the charioteer and his horses. You find it in the Bhagavad Gita, for example, and in Plato's *Phaedrus*. It symbolizes the state of balance, in which the horses (our instinctual, driven nature) are guided by the action of the reins (the will). The charioteer is calm, vigilant, and fully in charge, and brings under the unifying action of the will the manifold impulses and passions that, left to themselves, make life disorderly, contradictory, and unproductive.

In the Bhagavad Gita Krishna (who represents the Self), is the charioteer driving four white horses. He must help Arjuna (the human soul) face the battles of life instead of taking refuge in passivity and egoism. In Plato's *Phaedrus* the charioteer (the soul) travels across the cosmos, leading two horses. One tends toward heaviness and darkness, while the other toward the stars: the mission here is to regulate and discipline our manifold nature.

The task of self-mastery is arduous, but noble and fruitful. It is a necessary stage of our evolution. It is our lifetime task.

The Enigma of Time

What is our common experience of time? Sometimes we have too much of it, sometimes too little. Perhaps we have difficulty waiting, or have trouble finding the right rhythm. Or we put everything off to tomorrow. In rare moments, when immersed in beauty or love or awe, it feels as if time vanishes.

The more we think about time, the harder it is to understand it. In any case, it is useful and interesting to become familiar with this dimension: often we take it for granted and live without really being aware of it. If we feel comfortable with time, our ability for self-regulation can improve. Time is the field in which the will is made manifest.

Exercise

Think about what makes up an instant; about how now it exists, and now it does not. And yet that is all there is, because we are always in the present. Try to conceive and to catch a moment.

Do the same thing with a minute. How long is a minute? Let it pass, and observe all that happens inside yourself: thoughts, memories, sensations.

Think about a year. Where were you, how were you feeling one year ago? The concerns, projects, hopes of that day: what relevance do they have for you today?

Now think again about one year, but in the future. Another year of your life has passed. How are you situated in the future? How would you like to be a year from now?

Think about a million years, as far as your mind can, even remotely, conceive such a period of time. Think of the immensity of time.

Now try to conceive eternity: not as infinite time, but as the suspension of time. Have you ever momentarily experienced losing all sensation of time passing?

The first occasion in which you are impatient or rushed, expand your inner time. Try to think of a million years. Or cosmic time. Or eternity.

The first occasion in which you want to act without procrastinating, try to imagine the time between you and your action: How long is it? One minute? One month? One year? Then imagine reducing it to zero. Then do now what you were going to postpone.

PRACTICAL HINTS

Time is mysterious, maybe baffling. It is not easy to understand, and even less easy to deal with in a satisfactory way. Simply becoming familiar with this dimension, however, can be helpful.

Exploring mysteries, playing with enigmas: this is what inner work is often about.

AUTONOMY

Relying on Our Own Strengths

Vainamoinen the shaman was building a magnificent boat. He was creating it through the power of his song. But at some point he came to a deadlock. He was still missing three essential words. In order to know what they were, he had to go and ask Antero, a wizard endowed with secret powers.

When Vainamoinen reached Antero, he found a giant so still as to seem like a statue. Antero was lying down and looked dead. A tree was coming out of one shoulder, with squirrels running up and down on it, birds had made nests in his beard, his eyes were like stone. Vainamoinen asked for the three words, but got no answer. Yet he knew Antero was alive. After a while Vainamoinen slid inside Antero's mouth and fell into his stomach. There he grew a protective shell, and threatened the wizard, telling him he would not leave until he received what he wanted.

Vainamoinen vigorously kept demanding an answer, and provoked the giant wizard so that he would speak. In the end he obtained the three words. One gave him the secrets of nature, the second unraveled the enigma of life, and the third revealed to

*him the future. Now he knew the three words: he could finish
building his boat, freely navigate the seas, and reach the woman
he loved.*

—FINNISH MYTH

In many traditions we find a story of the hero who is swallowed by a monster or a great fish or a giant. After being inside for some time, he emerges, but is not the same as he was before. He has obtained new knowledge and strength. He has undergone an initiation. As Mircea Eliade has pointed out, these myths tell us that in the depths of our being live unimagined resources of spiritual energy and a secret knowing we usually neither explore nor express. Autonomy, in its full meaning, means the capacity to tap this extraordinary mine of wisdom and strength, without depending on others, without needing reassurance, entreaty, or protection.

Before exploring the theme of autonomy, let us establish a fact: To begin with, we human beings are *not* fully autonomous. On the contrary, we are dependent and vulnerable. Especially at the beginning and end of our life, we depend on the goodwill of others. During the rest of our life as well we depend on people we do not know for food and water, and for the normal functioning of society: electricity, traffic, hospitals, gas, mail, the Internet. We are not autonomous even from an internal, psychological point of view, because, be it in love or hate, in admiration or spite, we carry within us all the people who count in our life: "No man is an island."

In other words, we do not *have* interactions with others—we are *made* of interactions with others. We have survived through our long evolution because we are capable of helping and supporting one another. Each one of us is a microcosm in which humanity, in its entire history, is present. Complete autonomy or autarchy is a senseless, unthinkable pretense.

So why talk about autonomy? Because we can be more or less dependent—and the difference, even a small difference, means a lot for how we think and how we feel at each moment. Upon this trait rests the whole construction of our life. We have physical autonomy, except newborn babies, some of the elderly, and the disabled. But not all of us have emotional autonomy. Many people depend on other people's approval. They need others to lead them, help them, and hold their hand. They cannot be alone. Or perhaps they are dependent on a substance, gambling, the Internet, or alcohol; or they are compulsive shoppers. Just think of those who feel uneasy if their smartphone is turned off, or cannot leave the house without taking a drug, or need a drink to function in society, or must check their e-mails several times a day: people like us, maybe even ourselves, because we all have our weak points. Dependence is part of the human predicament.

Sometimes we say that a car has good autonomy. It means the gas tank is big and guarantees that the car can travel many miles. So it is with each of us. Our tank holds experiences, knowledge, resources, talents—and self-esteem. How big is it? Autonomy may be very limited—our mileage is low. It may seem to us that we cannot achieve much by ourselves; we think someone else ought to fill us up—imbue us with confidence, point the way, protect us, lead and advise us, even tell us how to think and which color tie to wear or what food to eat—as though we ourselves did not know.

Those who are instead more autonomous feel more at ease. They are able to think for themselves. They find within a raison d'être, so they are in touch with their own values and motivations. They do not need to consult an expert to know what they like or do not like. They do not pick up ideas as they come, but forge them with their thought. Often they appreciate solitude, because the time when they are alone is when they get their best insights.

All this is particularly true these days, in our extroverted society, which is vastly built on dependence. True, many people are recharged by others and get their best insights in collaboration and in the company of others. However, more than ever we neglect our need for silence and solitude—the best conditions for allowing original ideas to flower and for building inner strength. Go to a shopping mall and you will see crowds of people wandering in a subhypnotic state, looking for this or that stimulus: gadgets, clothing, food, music, films, anything at all to take them out of themselves. A harmless pastime, if it is counterbalanced by travel in inner space. We could almost say that the shopping mall is the materialized unconscious, a surreal world in which we roam around, ever distracted from ourselves, so near and yet so far from that sphere, which is really ever so close: our inner universe.

When we engage in full-time escapism, we cannot be in contact with ourselves, our true emotions and desires—as opposed to the artificial ones generated by the world of consumerism. It is no wonder that so many people are incapable of introspection, have lost contact with their own subjective world, and risk not knowing what they want, what intrigues them, who they are, and what is their life path.

The portrait of a dependent person is not a cheering one. In one way his life is easier—he is not accountable, and he is not fighting in the front line, but hands all responsibility over to the stronger and the wiser. The downside is a feeling dangerously akin to humiliation—because he is not fully using his resources. He does not have the satisfaction of being able to say, I can do it alone. Beneath dependency lies a sense of impotence and helplessness. And beneath that is the anger, often mute and imploded, of one who must submit to the circumstances of life and the will and whims of others.

Ralph Waldo Emerson wrote a wonderful essay on this subject: *Self-Reliance*. He believed that we do not trust our own ideas and therefore become other people's followers, only repeating what they have already said. The sign of true autonomy is to make room for what is hidden in us. And to think for ourselves—without following churches, parties, schools of thought, unless we have autonomously reflected on their tenets first. In the uncharted territory of your own thoughts, says

Emerson, ". . . you shall not discern the foot-prints of any other; you shall not see the face of man; you shall not hear any name; the way, the thought, the good, shall be wholly strange and new. It shall exclude example and experience."

A client of mine, Zelda, twenty years old, once said to me, with a nostalgic smile: "I miss myself." What does that mean? It means, I miss my world, the music I love, my photos and drawings and poetry. And why should you miss them? Because I do not have time, as I am busy with practical things. Indeed, everyone expects Zelda to make urgent decisions, and she is under pressure. The result is that her mood and self-esteem are suffering. Her situation improves straightaway if she allows herself a little attention for her world. Many of us find ourselves in this situation: we undervalue "our world"—our interests and capacities—in favor of duties and tasks we abhor. But in this way we cut ourselves off from a big part of our being: we are like someone who owns a magnificent palace, endowed with space, luxuries, and all kinds of conveniences, but uses only a dark, dusty storeroom in that building.

How can we hope to be strong if we are divorced from an essential part of ourselves? The remedy is often simple. We just ask ourselves: What do I really like? Where do I want to invest my vital energy? What qualities do I feel inside myself? What are my tastes and ideas? What are my strengths? No one can help us in this, for the simple reason that the answer must come from inside ourselves.

If we are not autonomous, we will feel dissonance at every moment of our life, because we will be forced to adhere to ideas that are not our own, adopt behaviors we would rather do without, and declare tastes that are foreign to us, because we have delegated to others the responsibility of choosing for us. Those who depend on approval and help from others feel constrained. It is as though they had to prove they are and always have been in line, because they feel their own ideas and actions have no intrinsic validity.

The quest for self-determination begins at birth. Every child puts her efforts into managing autonomously. The very impulse to be born originates in the baby. And just think of her joy at being able to walk unaided! We all remember our moments of autonomy: when we went to school by ourselves for the first time, for example; when we became economically independent; or when we went to live on our own. The conquest of autonomy gives vital energy and joy. Dependence may perhaps reassure us at first, but in the end it depresses us.

How do we acquire autonomy? There are no precise pointers. We will not find the "how" written anywhere. We have to find autonomy by ourselves. And there is no blueprint for conquering it. We invent and win it through hard effort—and by taking risks. Indeed, each step toward a new autonomy multiplies the probability of making mistakes.

When we seek our autonomy, it is inevitable that we make all kinds of blunders. But to make mistakes is an essential part of living. Think of all the autonomy you have gained: from when you started to eat with knife and fork instead of being spoon-fed, or day one at school, or when you began your first job, or your first important relationship. If I think of my own first conquests, they were studded with errors: the first time I crossed the road by myself I was almost run over by a big black car; soon after obtaining my driver's license, I got a fine; on my first trip abroad on my own, I ran out of money; in one of the very first lectures I gave, I was so boring and awkward that most of the audience walked out; one of my first psychotherapy clients followed me into the street and made a scene, yelling at me in public and tearing at her clothes, and I just stood there, not knowing what to do. Yet from each disaster I learned a lot.

What can greatly help in reaching autonomy is first of all to recall, one by one, our own gains, which certainly exist—and the small ones count, too. At one time or another even the least autonomous people have made some conquests. Furthermore, it helps to appreciate ourselves a bit more. For those with a background of constant self-deprecation, who continuously mull over their own failures, becoming more independent will be much more arduous.

In an Indian story, a man carries two jugs of water up a steep hill every day. They are suspended on a pole, which he carries on his shoulders. One of the jugs is new: it is very pleased with its own work, as it reaches the top of the hill without having lost a drop of water. The other jug has a crack, from which it drips, so that when it attains the end of the journey it is only half-full. This jug feels guilty because it wastes the water carrier's energy: much effort, little result. But after this activity has gone on for some time, it hears an inner voice saying: Look below! And the jug notices that beneath it the path is strewn with a trail of multicolored flowers, born of the water that, day after day, had accidentally dripped along the road.

The inferiority complex and self-pity, closely related to dearth of autonomy, are contingent on how we see and interpret ourselves and the world around us. We can learn to give a more open-minded and serene reading. An almost immediate consequence will be greater autonomy. Suppose our self-esteem is low. It will seem risky and stupid to turn to someone we do not esteem—that is, ourselves. And we are more likely to lean on someone we regard as more capable than we are. So at the basis of autonomy is a knowledge and familiarity with oneself, a clear appreciation of who we are and our worth.

Naturally we also have shortcomings; this does not have to be a reason for self-criticism. The most autonomous people face their deficiencies in three different ways: First, they develop capacities in fields where they feel strongest, just as a child who is not a star in sports will develop intellectual or artistic talents. Second, they cultivate the very area in which they feel lacking, as did Demosthenes, a stutterer who became a great orator. And third, as with the story of the two jugs, they see the hidden benefit of their weaknesses, like the psychotherapist who, because of his own hurt, develops an empathic sensitivity, which is at the heart of that work.

Autonomy is the nucleus of an act. Yet that nucleus may well be missing. Psychologists distinguish between an intrinsic motivation (I do something because I want to, and because it interests me) and an extrinsic motivation (I do it because I am made to by someone or something else). In an experiment on this theme, the subjects had to solve a puzzle (the Soma cube, which is composed of seven different parts that have to be reassembled in a cube or other shape: an intriguing puzzle that most consider a pleasant pastime). The experiment was carried out thus: In the first part, one group of subjects was asked to solve four configurations of the puzzle, and a second group was given the same task, but was paid to do it. After the sessions of both groups, there was an eight-minute break. During the break the subjects could do whatever they wanted: read magazines, do nothing—or keep playing with the cube. Unbeknownst to them, they were being observed, because this was the moment of interest to the researcher. How much time would the subjects spend playing with the cube during the break? This was a measure of motivation. Would the subjects who had previously been paid to play now start playing spontaneously and without being paid? The result was that the subjects who had *not* been paid were the ones most likely to play spontaneously, whereas the ones who *had* been paid, that is, prompted by an external motivation, were no longer interested when they were *not* paid. These subjects had lost not only their extrinsic motivation, but also their intrinsic one! In other words, when an extrinsic motivation is given, the intrinsic one falls. Stop the pay, stop the play.

To put this another way, if we give a child a bicycle, book, or guitar, it may interest her, and she may try to learn it and apply herself to do so. If we promise her a reward, such as a sweet or money, so that she learns it more quickly, she will probably try harder there and then; but when the reward is suspended, her interest in the bicycle, book, or guitar falls: where is my money?

The experiment was repeated in many variations. For instance, instead of money, the experimenters promised success: let us see who is best at solving puzzles. Competition, too, diminished intrinsic motivation—subjects lost interest. The same goes for time limits, evaluations, and active supervision. Any kind of pressure, even masked pressure, emptied the intrinsic motivation. (What does all this remind you of? Read the next paragraph!)

Edward Deci, creator of this experiment, maintains that controlling people reduces their self-determination. If I choose an activity because it interests me, I have the feeling of being in control, and place more value on what I do. But if I am directed from the outside, the feeling of alienation grows. We enjoy the feeling of being the cause of our own actions, not pawns moved by external forces. This discovery is of huge importance for every field of human activity and expression. First and foremost, school, given that our schools function primarily on the principle of extrinsic motivation: marks, teachers' reproaches, punishment, and parents' reactions, all of which make students more dependent, and less interested in what they are studying. In short, these parameters are an organized training in lack of autonomy. The more teachers go along with their students' interests and convey the meaning and beauty in their studies, the more likely they engender *lifelong learning* (LLL): a student continues to learn and be interested in all kinds of subjects even after school finishes, indeed for the rest of her life.

Notably, many of the great educators fully realized the importance of autonomy in a child's or student's education. Respect for the child's autonomy runs through all of Maria Montessori's work: for her, independence is the basis of freedom. One must not help a child do anything he can learn to do himself, whether it is walking, dressing, using a spoon or fork to feed herself, etc. Of course it is quicker if we dress a child, but if instead we let him learn for himself, we respect his dignity and encourage his independence. Thus Alison Stallibrass suggested development through free play. In her Pioneer Centre, children were free to choose the games they wanted to play, without any direction, without anyone introducing rewards or punishments, or organizing contests to further competitiveness. They played for the sake of playing, without being interrupted, spontaneously organizing themselves, and so cultivated their autonomy.

The Sudbury Valley School in Framingham, Massachusetts, was established on this very basis. The theory is that you learn much more when you are motivated to learn and decide independently what and when to study. Learning then takes on all the spontaneity and lightness of play. School decisions are made democratically in meetings where all present have the right to vote. Teachers are available for assisting students on demand. It would seem a dangerous and odd initiative. But the results are good and the students go through to university and find work. Meanwhile, they learn to be free and autonomous.

A concept parallel to that of intrinsic and extrinsic motivation is locus of control. Who is controlling our life? If, as a student, I fail an exam, will I take responsibility and say it was because I did not study enough and did not prepare properly; or will I say that it is the teacher's fault—he is a fascist who just likes to pick on me? If the relationship with my husband is not working, will I blame him for not listening to me, or not pulling his weight, or always being grumpy? Or will I take (at least in part) responsibility for what is happening?

Clearly, an internal locus that is overdeveloped will tend to make us feel omnipotent or plague us with feelings of guilt. But to recognize that we are responsible for our attitudes, opinions, and choices makes us more independent and therefore freer. We are no longer the victims of events we cannot control. Here, too, it is a question of different readings of the events in our life. In one case we are at the mercy of forces over which we are powerless: this is the main cause of stress and depression. In the other we find ourselves responsible for how we think and behave. Various studies have found that discovering one's own responsibility is one of the most important features of successful psychotherapy.

I shall now tell you a story about the conquest of autonomy. A student of mine, Emma, one day came to a session rather alarmed: "No one told me it was going to snow!" It was only sleet for the time being, but her anxiety had some cause. My studio is in the hills, and going back down in the snow can be tricky. In Emma's hometown she had never driven a car. Any affirmation of feminine independence is regarded with suspicion. But Emma is an intelligent woman with a rich inner world. For her, learning to drive was a milestone on her way to autonomy. From the start of the session I felt she had something to tell me, but was hesitating. At some point she said, "I have to talk to you." Meanwhile, through the window I could see the snow was now falling heavily in large flakes. Emma said, "I want to change therapists." Understandably I was sorry to hear this. Individual work is a momentous journey that crosses chasms, peaks, wasteland, and stupendous landscapes. In our school it takes at least four years. Emma was not happy with our work together and felt blocked. She decided she wanted the very best for herself, and it seemed to her I could not offer what she expected. Naturally her words hurt my ego—I admitted it, to myself and to her: You mean I am not the best? But at the same time a signal lit up in my brain, the one that tells me when someone is taking a step forward in her growth. My instinct told me that some serious progress was going on. And indeed it was. For Emma this was a step closer to her autonomy. To tell me she wanted the best, and that I was not the best, was for her an arduous task. It was hard for her to affirm herself—and with a man in position of authority, harder still. You never know: I might have gotten upset and sent her away (that was a fantasy of hers), she might not have found another teacher. To part ways with me was a big decision. What is more, she was afraid of offending me. She was scared to speak clearly and directly. It was easier for her to express herself by manipulation and allusion, but gradually she gave up these indirect modes of communication. To affirm a deep need of hers—wanting the best for her inner life and her growth—was sacrosanct, but acknowledging her own needs was for her a huge conquest. Now she was doing it.

Emma was learning to move outside the lines, to follow her own judgments, and not those of others, and to listen to her inner voice. At the end of the session she was satisfied. The details of her decision were not yet clear, but anyhow she had said what she wanted to say. Meanwhile, the snowfall had become even heavier. But Emma felt able to face it without anxiety, with full autonomy. And so she went out into the blizzard.

Our conquest of autonomy need not be at the cost of our relations with others. Parallel to our wish for autonomy, self-realization, and expression is another, equally important tendency: the need to belong to something greater than ourselves and enter into a relationship with others, to nourish and be nourished, and to love. The wish to be entirely self-sufficient, and the dream of being complete by ourselves and never needing others, is destined for a sad future. We become rigid and haughty, unable to let go, ridiculously self-important. Yet again the Greek myths warn us. Think of Icarus. He wanted to go it alone, and ended up at the bottom of the sea.

Furthermore, we must seek autonomy only when we are ready: it must not be imposed. We need patience and humility to respect the pace of maturing. In natural life, of which we are part, we find that processes mature slowly. This reality is often forgotten. We have surely sometimes found ourselves holding a green banana or a rock-hard peach—the products of refrigeration—foods alienated from their natural rhythm. The same disregard can apply to human beings. Thus you find, for example, children forced to walk when they should be crawling; little girls who seem miniature women; young boys driving a car, although they have not learned the lessons of practical judgment and respect for others; people of all ages driven to decisions for which they do not feel ready. Remember Kazantzakis's butterfly? A man tries to help a butterfly come out of its cocoon, with the result that the butterfly, having emerged too soon, is unable to fly.

Let us return to our initial point: the discovery that within us we have a resource of wisdom and strength that we usually do not tap, but that, on the contrary, is left forgotten in a remote part of ourselves. We might visualize it as a character: an individual who is not upset by the dramas of everyday life; he, or she, sees the big picture; knows and loves the splendor of wild nature, the exquisiteness of flowers, the awesome beauty of the sea and the starry skies. This person has an ancient, benevolent wisdom, and a healthy dose of cosmic humor.

We may have lost touch with our own innate wisdom, and therefore feel inadequate, lost, fragile, and incapable. But we can reinstate the contact. In my workshops I ask participants to meet a Wise Old Man or Wise Old Woman, and to ask this character the important questions in our life they want answers to. Responses often come, and with them, an influx of energy and greater clarity. The answer is never flat and on the same level as the question, but gives a new perspective and a new insight. We obtain a different point of view, perhaps a surprising one, and a confidence we did not have before.

One time when I was leading this exercise in the United States, I asked group participants to meet their wise *being*: I did not want to emphasize male or female. But because of my faulty pronunciation, many understood it as "wise bean," whom they then obediently met. And guess what happened: they received much wise advice and enlightening tips anyway. It seems the wise bean worked just as well as the wise person. Because I believed (and still do) in the power of symbolic images, this was a disconcerting state of affairs. It appeared that images were interchangeable, since the end result was the same. I then realized that the deep attitude was even more important than the symbols themselves: to bet, and then discover, that we have within us the answers we seek, the strength necessary to tackle the obstacles we run into, and also a wisdom and a depth we did not know we had. That is autonomy.

Inventory of Resources

One of the most common observations you can make in psychotherapy is that people do not know their own value; they concentrate on their mistakes, deficiencies, and problems; or they delude and overestimate themselves. Both these tendencies cause all kinds of trouble.

Autonomy is based on a realistic knowledge of one's own resources, and on their full expression.

To know, own, and express all that is valuable and helpful in yourself is not hard. All you need is a little faith and the willingness to try.

Contact with your own strengths is a necessary condition for activating the will.

Exercise

Make a list of your qualities (for example, enthusiasm, truthfulness, patience, etc.) and your abilities (for example, speaking Russian, or baking cakes). Include also the resources that show up only occasionally, or those that are partial or potential. Be neither modest nor presumptuous.

Take qualities and abilities, one at a time, and analyze them thoroughly. How have they enriched your life and that of others? Let memories emerge of these qualities or abilities being expressed, and having an effect. Would you like to express them more fully?

Enter into closer contact with a resource from your list. How do you experience it in yourself? Does it have an emotional tone, a specific presence? Let a symbolic image for this resource appear: an animal, a flower, a tree, a character, an object, whatever arises naturally from deep within the psyche.

Proceed in the same way with the other resources on your list.

PRACTICAL HINTS

It is important to ask yourself: To what extent have I realized these qualities and abilities? Do they belong only to my inner world, so that I alone know of them, or have they some effect on the world around me? If they are not manifest in my concrete life or that of others, it is as if they did not exist. They are like a seed that has not yet germinated.

DEPTH

Finding the Vein of Gold

The philosopher Zhong Li met a hunchback who was catching cicadas. He was amazingly skillful, using a long pole to catch one after another. Zhong Li was impressed: "How did you become so clever? Do you have a technique?" The hunchback answered yes: For months he had practiced holding in perfect balance a pole with a ball on it. Then he did it with two balls, one on top of the other. Then with three, and finally with five. But the most important secret was his total concentration on what he wanted to achieve: "In the immensity of the universe and the multiplicity of things, I think of nothing but the cicadas; I neither turn nor bend. I would not swap the wings of a cicada for everything in the world. How then could I not catch them?"

Zhong Li concluded: "Concentration of spirit makes one like a god."

—CHUANG TZU

C hances are you are not interested in catching cicadas. But this is in fact a matter that concerns everyone, because it pertains to the depth at which we meet the various circumstances of our existence. Chuang Tzu, the Taoist philosopher, held great admiration for people with exceptional skills. He thought they were in touch with a vital secret: the butcher who for nineteen years did not sharpen his knife (his colleagues did so every month) because he moved it in the empty interspaces of the meat he was cutting; the old man who would dive into a river in flood and calmly emerge as from a pleasant swim; the carpenter who studied the shapes of trees and was absorbed by his art to the point of forgetting all worldly concerns. And there was also the archer, able to shoot one arrow after another without spilling a drop from a flask of water poised on his elbow—even when he stood on a rock above a precipice. My favorite is the painter who was asked by a prince to paint a crab. "I need a villa with twelve servants, and five years' time," replied the painter. The prince agreed, and after five years sent his messengers to obtain the fin-ished product. But nothing had been done yet. "I need five more years," said the painter. The prince agreed. However, he re-marked that it would have to be a really beautiful crab. After this period, the messengers went back. But the painter had still not done anything. Then suddenly he took his brush, and in a few moments painted the most beautiful crab ever created by human hand.

These stories have a common element: behind excellence of any kind lies a long practice with the material, undivided attention, and the ability to become one with the task at hand. This is depth: the capacity to enter a subject and find in it a whole universe. It is the same for every subject. For instance, you can use music as a ring tone for a cell phone or whistle it absentmindedly. You can listen to it attentively. You can master it through study, and play it on an instrument. You can perform it before an audience. You can explore it in its huge, perhaps infinite, richness of meaning and nuance.

It may not be easy to practice depth. Our mind wanders: that is its nature. This tendency is accentuated by the hurried and distracted times we live in. A farmer in the Middle Ages may have had to struggle with famine, invasions, exploitation, or drought. But his life was simple, with few factors at play. People in the twenty-first century are in another condition altogether. We are more protected materially (in the wealthier societies). But the world we inhabit is vastly more complex. Every day a profusion of stimuli reaches us. The electronic messages we receive and send keep us busy. The pace is ever faster, duties more numerous. Our mind must tackle not only our own predicament, but also the difficulties and anguish of the world: an earthquake in Turkey or a flood in the Pacific basin, a financial crisis or a new global virus, climate change or youth unemployment. At the same time we are enticed by countless promises of pleasure: food, elegance, technology, sex.

We are invaded, confused, distracted. A well-known study

shows that if people at the entrance of a supermarket are offered three free samples of jam of brand X, they are more likely to buy that same brand of jam later. If they are instead offered a choice among twenty-four free samples, the persuasive strength is much lower, because the potential buyers are confused and overstimulated. We find the same happens with children. Show them three toys, and they will know what to choose: but offer them twenty-four and they grow restless. These experiments symbolize the human condition in our century. Because we are surrounded by an overabundance of stimuli, we become restless and scattered. Ultimately this state becomes a way of being, so that it is no longer seen as a discomfort, but taken for granted because it is common and universally shared. It is the constant background to our every thought and action.

Consider the scenario: a person in the twenty-first century is intent on some project or other, and a text message arrives, or the phone rings, either of which, with its bizarre and insistent tone, interrupts the continuity of her thoughts. The ideas and the stimuli circulating on the Internet or in the newspapers or on television capture her for a moment: a lottery, a sports record, a mysterious murder, some tabloid gossip, a political scoop. But straightaway another stimulus comes and grabs her attention. The quiet relationship with books is for many an old-fashioned pastime—we now move with the fast, uneven pace of links and hypertexts. Relationships with others multiply, yet grow increasingly lightweight and empty. How many friends do you have on Facebook who you have perhaps never met?

According to one English statistic, three out of five couples break up by SMS. How two people end a relationship says a lot about that relationship. The final phase sums up and symbolizes the whole affair. Separating via smartphone means (I suspect) being unable to look one another in the eyes and say what is important, not having the courage to face the other's reaction, and not jumping together into the stormy seas of deep emotions. A distracted, hurried relationship.

Today's world is extraordinary for the possibilities it offers. But the risks it exposes us to are great, and superficiality is one of the greatest. The dweller of modernity often lives a life made up of friends he does not know, ideas he has not examined in depth, non-places without a history, pleasures sensed but not fully relished, love not experienced with the heart and soul. And he either is, or risks becoming, an absentminded android living a fragmented, unfulfilling life.

Depth, on the other hand, is a strength. To be deep, we must resist intimidation or distraction. We must go through boredom and insecurity, preserve our motivation, and tolerate emptiness—all without being sidetracked or discouraged. Only then will our relationship disclose its beauty; only then will the subject we are studying show us its richness of meaning; only then will the project we have begun—whether it's preparing for a holiday or writing a symphony—start to bear fruits.

Let us see how it works. A story from Jewish tradition will help. There was once a student who very much wanted to study the Talmud. He went to a rabbi who was well known for his ability to interpret this great body of sacred writing, and asked to become his pupil. "I don't think that is possible," said the rabbi. "I am afraid you lack the right attitude. And then, you need constancy to understand the true meaning of the Talmud." "What is the right attitude?" "It is impossible to describe, but if you like, I can present you with three riddles. If you solve them, it means you have the potential, and I will take you as my pupil." The young man accepts the challenge, and the rabbi starts with the first riddle: "Two chimney sweeps go inside a chimney full of soot to clean it. When they come out, one has a dirty face, the other a clean one. Which one washes his face?" "That's easy," answers the student, "the one with the dirty face." "Not so, the one with the clean face. He sees that the other has a dirty face, thinks his face is dirty, too, and washes it." "Ask me the second riddle." "Here it is: Two men go inside a sooty chimney to clean it. When they come out, one has a dirty face, the other a clean one. Who washes his face?" "But this is the same as the first riddle! You have already told me the answer: the one with the clean face." "Not so," said the rabbi. "The answer is: the one with the dirty face. Let me explain. The one with the clean face tells the other, Do I have a dirty face, too? The other replies no, he does not, but because of this question he realizes *he* has a dirty face, and washes it." "All right," said the student. "Let's see if I can at least solve the third riddle." "Here it is: Two men go into a sooty chimney to clean it. When they come out, one has a dirty face, the other a clean one. Who washes his face?" "I won't be fooled this time! I bet they both wash their faces." "Not so. The bottom line is, the whole story does not make sense. How can two people go into a sooty chimney and emerge from it, one with a dirty face and the other with a clean one? Clearly they both must have dirtied their faces. The point here is that you always have to look at the context and challenge the assumptions!" The student is most discouraged: "I did not solve even one riddle. So I cannot become your pupil." "On the contrary: you already are. Just look at how far we have come. The crucial learning point here is that you can see the same question from many perspectives, and that fully understanding any subject takes a good deal of work."

There you have depth: not stopping at the first impression, but reflecting, digging, changing your point of view, persevering. Reality is manifold and unpredictable: to understand it, you have to insist. In human relations, in learning, in almost any enterprise, in all aspects of life, if you do not look in depth, you miss the essence.

Take the story of Agassiz. A student introduces himself to Louis Agassiz, professor of zoology at Harvard University. "I want to study with you," he says. He is interested in insects. Agassiz instead gives him a fish preserved in alcohol and asks him to observe it attentively. The student is a bit disappointed—fish are not his favorite subject—but he sets to work. After ten minutes he thinks he has observed all there is to see. After an hour he is bored with the glassy stare of the fish, and the professor is nowhere to be seen, so he decides to go home. In the afternoon he goes back to his fish. As there is nothing else to do, he starts looking at it again—he studies the teeth, the scales. Then he draws it, and in drawing it he finds new details he had not noticed before. The professor returns and asks the student to describe what he has observed: the holes on the head, the eyes without lids, the fringed gills, the mobile operculum, the forked tail, etc. But the professor is unsatisfied: "You have not noticed the most important item," he says. The student is again left alone with his fish.

The young man decides really to go for it, and discovers a series of details he had not noticed before. Yet he still does not understand what the most relevant aspect is. The professor sends him home and tells him to come back the next morning. During the night the student wakes up with an intuition: the most important characteristic of the fish is that its structure has symmetrical, paired organs. Conscientious observation has borne fruits. Now the student believes he has finished—but no, he is just at the beginning. The professor asks him to keep studying the subject for another three days. The fourth day he gives him another specimen of the same kind of fish—a *Haemulon*—and tells him to study the differences between the two. The study then continues for the next eight *months*, broadening to other fish, and what the student previously loathed is now arousing his interest. Without ever looking at an insect, the student has had the best lesson in entomology. Now he is able to see; he knows how to observe and study. When you plunge into the depths, any subject becomes fascinating. Even a dead fish.

By deepening our search, we can understand better; we acquire mastery and gain confidence; we most likely develop a more perceptive relationship with the subject studied; we grow stronger; we enrich our experience.

At this point enters K. Anders Ericsson, a Swedish psychologist. For thirty years he has studied talent and exceptional performance. His main finding is that at the core of excellence is not innate talent but intelligent perseverance. Ericsson studied golfers, typists, nurses, violinists, dart throwers, Scrabble players, basketball players, computer programmers, and others who showed uncommon abilities in their field. He studied them from various points of view: how they reached success, their teachers or mentors, the quality of their memory, their attitude toward failure, their methods of daily practice, the amount of study, etc. He concluded that there is no evidence of innate talent—exceptional performance comes through years of hard work. Ericsson coined the term "deliberate practice," which does not consist in mechanical repetition of a gesture (throwing the ball into the basket or playing scales on the piano). Rather it consists in assiduous practice based on intelligent repetition, immediate feedback (that is, recognizing straightaway any progress or any step backward), awareness of one's own weak points and healthy self-criticism, constant effort to overcome one's limits, and the passionate striving for excellence. This is why, says Ericsson, we have to dedicate ourselves to what inspires us the most. Only in this way will we find the strength to persevere for many years. Studies that entirely rule out innate talent, and that band together activities as diverse as throwing darts and playing the violin, may arouse some doubts. Nevertheless they provide valuable evidence in favor of hard work and persistence. They cannot be ignored, and are surely most encouraging for anyone who is ready to knuckle down.

There is also a series of studies by Angela Duckworth et al., who concentrated on *grit* (meaning passion and perseverance invested in a long-term goal). These studies, using various techniques, have investigated thousands of people of different ages and backgrounds. Again, the result was clear: grit is an essential factor in success, and is an even better predictor of professional success than IQ.

At the core of depth you can find an element of unyielding strength, and readiness to take on any obstacle. After a while we meet a death in some form—in the sense of blind alley, confusion, defeat, or disintegration. That is when we vacillate. We feel discouraged. We have thoughts such as "I can't do this," "There's no point going on," "This is not for me," "I ought to throw in the towel." But this happens in any worthwhile venture. Only after a "death" can we fully understand the nature of a relationship or a subject of study. Only then will we have deepened our emotional commitment and harnessed our latent resources. Only then have we truly had the chance to comprehend, because we have gone in deep enough.

The deep attitude is first of all cognitive. It entails a flexible, multifaceted use of the mind; it is emotional, because it draws on layers of the psyche otherwise left dormant, such as trust, the thrill of risking, the joy of success, and the motivation for exploring diverse and unpredictable scenarios, unknown to those who stay on the surface. It is also volitional: with the will we decide to go on, to endure boredom, to deepen even when it seems as if there is nothing to deepen, to stand firm when weariness or desperation urge us to give up.

Depth is the very essence of education. As most educators know, learning can be superficial or in-depth. The first way of learning is exterior. The heart does not participate. We learn by rote, and the basic criterion is testing: we have to pass an exam—knowledge is conceived as a measurable value. It is external and instrumental: external, because students do not experience this knowledge as part of their own inner being; and instrumental, because the student's sole or main aim is not to gain knowledge, but to pass an exam.

In-depth learning is the opposite: it is internal, since students who go in for it participate actively in the process. They understand the full import of the subject they are studying, penetrate it, and make it their own, have a passion for it, and can apply it to their life, linking it to other, prior, learning. Above all, whatever they learn, they feel intimately related to their inner world.

We can also see it in terms of the consumer versus in-depth approach. As consumers, we want a product, but after a while get rid of it, because that object no longer has the vibrancy and freshness it had when it was brand-new. A consumer wants a relationship with a person, but expends him like popcorn or a soft drink. She does not receive that person's deep essence, which is gleaned after years of shared experience, but limits herself to immediate enjoyment—a superficial and hurried episode. This is a dangerously negligent way to treat any person or topic of study or even a physical object. The consumer attitude is one of the most deleterious aspects that the spirit of modernity—though dynamic and manifold—has brought with it.

The big hurdle here is that our precious tool, the mind, while capable of depth, can also be easily distracted or divided or invaded by parasites of every kind. In an example from Ramakrishna, two friends meet and realize they have two very different plans for the evening: "I will enjoy myself in the company of beautiful women," says one; "I will go to the temple to pray," says the other. After they part, each proceeds as planned. But the one who likes women thinks, Maybe I would have been better off going to the temple; the one who was going to pray is continually distracted by the thought, women would have been more fun.

To get around the problem of superficiality and distraction, there is only one remedy: develop perseverance and concentration. A great poem from Islamic culture has clothed this teaching with beauty and a good dose of irony. It is Attar's *Conference of the Birds*. Birds from all over the world are in crisis: they are confused, have lost all inner security, and urgently need guidance. They all meet to decide how to go about it. One of them, the hoopoe, says he knows of an extraordinary bird, the Simurg, who will be able to pull them out of their predicament and wisely guide them to fulfillment. They can go to him together, but the journey is long and dangerous. Some birds react straightaway:

the sparrow says he does not feel up to it, the owl is too attached to his possessions, the peacock is too much in love with himself, the falcon wants to be the boss, and so on. These birds impersonate our most common resistances to full commitment. Then some birds, the strongest and most decisive, set off in flight. The journey is long and they must cross many perilous places: the initial selection is just a foretaste of what happens next. Thousands of birds get lost or die on the way.

The survivors have to cross seven valleys. The journey of the birds is in fact our own journey, complex and demanding. First we find the Valley of Search, where, after hardship and suffering, we make our first discoveries. Then we reach the Valley of Love, where we learn to give up caution, since love is by definition an adventure. Other valleys await us: the Valley where the Mystery is glimpsed, but the way multiplies into infinite paths, as each traveler has to find the one that is his own; the Valley of Detachment, where we face paradoxes and contradictions—an ant is equal to an elephant, and the whole of humanity counts as much as a drop of water—here we must detach from our stereotypes and thinking habits; the Valley of Unity, where we learn to understand that each entity contains in itself the whole world, and that each person comprises all the others; the Valley of Confusion, where all that we have learned up to now does not count anymore; and finally the Valley of Nothingness, where we drink at the cup of oblivion and meet face-to-face with the ineffable, that which no word can really express.

In the end the birds—only thirty are left—fly on to meet

the Simurg: they have made it. They are overjoyed. They have reached the Simurg—the fullness of being. What is curious is that in ancient Persian, "thirty birds" is pronounced *si-murg*. The thirty birds who have made this long and arduous journey to a faraway land, and at the end have found what they wanted most of all in the universe, had been at all times infinitely close to their goal. In fact, they *are* the Simurg. They have reached an alien world, and have discovered there what is most familiar. They have traveled for years, far from all they knew, to arrive in the end at the very center of their inner world.

The teaching of this ancient text is of huge value. When we devote ourselves to a project, a relationship, an activity, or learning, the depth we reach will allow us to find ourselves. In our project we find who we are. In the person closest to us, if we have truly deepened the relationship through all the differences and difficulties, we find our own true being. This means that we find out what stuff we are made of and what we are capable of feeling and knowing and doing. Instead, if we let ourselves be carried here and there by the whims of life, if we allow our path to be interrupted, if we tire and give up, at the end all we feel is fragmentation and dissatisfaction. We will feel that we have wasted the day—or our life. How we handle any project or relationship fundamentally determines and colors what we feel we are.

We find ourselves, because we have invested our whole being, with no compromises or reservations. Indeed, besides perseverance, depth requires commitment—the ability to be fully involved. In working day after day with individuals struggling with their choices, I have seen over and over two basic attitudes in any human enterprise. One is self-protective and cautious, such as in those who wade carefully into the water, one toe first; who are involved in a relationship but dream of another one; who read a book, while wondering what is on television; who work, but prefer to be on holiday. There is always a "but": a reservation, a hidden back door through which they can always exit and go elsewhere.

The other attitude is held by those who are ready to make a bet and put themselves on the line. Risk is ever present; it is the possibility of failure, ridicule, or humiliation—or just plain wasting time. If you give a project—or a person—everything you have got, you can lose your bet. A margin of uncertainty is ever present. Of course, we wish for absolute certainty. It is mostly a vain hope, because whatever our choice may be, we will never have all possible information available. Something can always go wrong. We are necessarily in the condition of having to risk, placing our bet and then waiting to see. There are no guarantees.

The Bhagavad Gita, the wonderful classic of the Indian spiritual tradition, begins with two armies confronting each other. The two ranks of heavily deployed forces face one another. Dressed in a multitude of colors, the soldiers line up, holding their weapons. Tension fills the air. The drums roll, the war trumpets sound. The battle is about to start. But Arjuna, the main character, does not want to fight. He draws back, hesitates.

Discouraged, he throws down his bow and gives up. At this point Krishna, who represents the spiritual Self, exhorts him to enter the fray. He explains that life and death are nothing other than a play of the mind, and Arjuna need not fear. Self-realization comes only from full, courageous engagement. Arjuna must involve himself: that is what he decides to do.

Arjuna's situation is one we all share: sometimes we are reluctant, and for fear of being hurt, we do not commit ourselves totally, but delegate all action to a kind of alter ego of ourselves, which diligently carries out the moves it must make, whatever they may be. It makes love, but is not wholly present. It studies, but without soul. It goes to work, but could not really care less. Because it does not give of itself, it does not receive anything in return.

We can describe it in economic terms: spending, saving, wasting. To reach depth, we must expend ourselves. Sometimes this means we must expose ourselves, make mistakes, waste time, fail.

Excessive saving of oneself consists in not using our faculties to their fullest, but in giving ourselves over to meaningless thoughts and actions. It is a solution that may offer momentary and fictitious relief, but ends up generating uneasiness and disorientation. True, at times hesitating or protecting ourselves, even being suspicious, can save our life. But if we become chronically unable to commit, then we end up nowhere.

The paradox here is that by saving, we end up wasting. We

draw back to protect ourselves, but in so doing, we miss the opportunity life presents at that moment.

To sum up: Depth is a quality that is hard to define or quantify. In it there is a healthy dose of persistence and passion and the capacity for not giving up when the going gets rough. It involves every aspect of our existence: work, relationships, intellectual and spiritual life. To have a *unifying center* in our life has a beneficial effect, because it organizes all the components of our psyche, which would otherwise be dissipated chaotically. As when a magnet placed over iron filings creates orderly patterns, so does a unifying center give cohesion and strength to our personality. In a disorderly and distracted psyche, pathology can much more easily put down roots. Often the most effective remedy for depression, anxiety, obsessions, and phobias is not reached through elaborate techniques, but in pursuing a strong interest that can act as unifying theme. Depth heals us and regenerates us. Superficiality, scatteredness, and emptiness, instead, open the doors to pathology. In working with my psychotherapy clients, I have ascertained time and again that to immerse ourselves in a new project—doing volunteer work, learning to play a musical instrument, starting a commercial activity, a new relationship, even simply reading a book—can have far more beneficial effects than some specific medicine or technique.

The secret is just that: Instead of skimming the surface, we dig deep. When we find stones, we do not stop there. Continuing to dig, we will discover the vein of gold.

The Art of Reflection

To reflect is to deepen. To think repeatedly about a subject helps us understand it. If we persevere, if we examine it in its various aspects and from different points of view, we will know it more intimately; we will be able to immerse ourselves in that subject and comprehend it.

This way of thinking is the opposite of the fleeting and superficial wandering that is currently so common. Our thinking is often hurried and scattered. We urgently need to learn the art of reflection.

In reflecting deeply we activate the will as self-discipline and perseverance.

Exercise

Choose a quality (for example, love, beauty, honesty) as a focus for reflection (the same technique can be adapted, with small, appropriate changes, to any subject you want to explore: a person, a project, a situation).

Think of the quality you have chosen. By way of example, let's say it is love. How many kinds and varieties of love can you think of? What effects do they have? What are their main characteristics? What are their benefits? What are their possible dangers? What memories do you have about this quality—in yourself and in others?

Imagine a knob, like the volume control on a radio. You can increase or decrease this quality, in yourself and around you, and in the world. What effects would this operation have? What would your life be like if there were more—or less—of this quality?

Consider your mental assumptions in thinking about this quality. Now turn them upside down, or at any rate begin to question them. What if the opposite of all you had thought until now were true?

Let analogies and symbols come to mind regarding this quality. Can you come up with a metaphor?

Think of absurd and paradoxical situations. For example, is it possible to love your own enemies?

Create some "thought experiments," imaginary scenarios in which to deliberately experiment with new attitudes and behaviors.

Change perspective. How would an astronaut perceive this quality? Or a poet? A farmer? Someone from a faraway culture, or a different epoch, or another planet? Or you—at a different stage of your life?

PRACTICAL HINTS

It is important not to stop reflecting too soon. Sometimes we seem to have exhausted a subject, when really we are just beginning. We have to keep going even when it may appear we have finished. If we continue without being discouraged, new ideas and surprising scenarios may soon emerge.

RESILIENCE

Renewal after Adversity

The old donkey did not have much longer to live.

He had worked all his life, day after day serving the master with constancy and loyalty. But the master was not grateful: why on earth should he thank a beast? He saw that the old donkey was of no more use. The time had come to get rid of him. So he took him to an abandoned well. The donkey was calm and trusting. It was easy to push him in. The master threw in a few shovelfuls of earth, and that was that.

Well, not quite. The master had already started homeward when he heard a voice from the bottom of the well: "Can I have a bit more dirt?"

Surprised, the master went back to see. He looked into the well, and soon his eyes became accustomed to the dark. The donkey's voice reached his ears: "I need a bit more dirt to climb up. Each time you throw it in, I shake it off, then climb onto it, trample it down, and so I am a bit closer to the top.

"So, when are you going to throw me some more?"

—MIDDLE EASTERN STORY

The old donkey gives us a fine display of resilience—the ability, under difficult, perhaps dramatic, circumstances, to react with strength and confidence. In cases of natural disasters, financial crisis, illness, persecution, war, poverty, discomfort, and mishap of any kind, resilience means we do not succumb to hindrances and misfortunes, but face them realistically and constructively; it pulls us out of troublesome situations and allows us to help others, too. The word comes from Latin and refers to metals. It means "to resume the original form after undergoing percussion." To be resilient means being able to get up after falling, or, after suffering adverse circumstances, to bounce back stronger than before.

Some of us are more resilient than others. One of the first studies of this trait was done on children who had been victims of abuse. For a majority of them, their hurt was so deep that it caused serious chronic difficulties for the rest of their lives. But about one-third of these children developed a series of characteristics—adaptation to adverse circumstances, friendships with peers, ability to relate well to adults, school success, self-affirmation—all of which made them *above average*, indeed, exceptional children. They have been called "the invulnerables."

Another study—on children from the island of Kauai, reared by parents who were psychotic or alcoholic—found that some of them had an extraordinary capacity for reacting to adverse circumstances by developing inner strength and determination. A study conducted on sons and daughters of Vietnamese immigrants to the United States reached similar conclusions. Under dramatic circumstances, they had been forced to leave their homes and country. When they arrived in America, they had only the clothes they were wearing, and spoke only their native tongue. Here, too, a percentage of them not only adapted, but attained levels of excellence.

The same happened in the Sichuan region in China, hit in the year 2008 by an earthquake that claimed 70,000 victims. Soon after the catastrophe, the survivors began reconstruction. What saved them was solidarity, as well as a readiness to do here and now whatever had to be done, without falling prey to the demons of discouragement and sorrow.

Yet another example is that of the boys from South Sudan, between seven and seventeen years of age, who were forced by tragedy to leave their country during the civil war. While they were out looking after their cattle, their families had been exterminated. To survive, they had to flee immediately to Ethiopia, walking across wild, uninhabited land. This was the fate of about 20,000 kids. They set off with nothing; many died of hunger and thirst, or were mauled by lions. Others survived.

Cities, too, can be resilient. One study focuses on the many cities that in the course of history have been destroyed by war or natural catastrophe. The overwhelming majority have been rebuilt: San Francisco after the earthquake and fire in 1906; Hiroshima and Nagasaki after nuclear destruction; Dresden after the firebombing in World War II; Goma, in the Congo, after being completely destroyed by a volcanic eruption in September 2001. Naturally, it was not the cities themselves that had been resilient, but the inhabitants, who, after the terrible misfortune of seeing their world suddenly disappear, after the grief over losing loved ones, together set out to rebuild their city from scratch.

Resilience is by no means guaranteed. After a trauma, some fall and do not get up. Some carry the consequences of their wounds for the rest of their lives. Wearily and bitterly, they trudge and limp along until the day they die. This is precisely why studying resilience and learning how it can be cultivated is so urgent.

I have had the good fortune to know several people endowed with great resilience. For example, my aunt Laura Archera Huxley, during World War II went to the United States, where she gave her debut performance at Carnegie Hall in New York as violin soloist in Mozart's Fifth Violin Concerto. She was about to take the ship back to Italy. But when she was about to embark, a half hour before sailing, she received a telegram from her father—my future grandfather: *Do not leave.* Hitler was bombing civilian passenger ships in the Atlantic! My aunt had just enough time to take her luggage and get off. She stood alone on the wharf; in those few moments, her life had completely changed. Officially regarded by the United States as an enemy alien (at the time Italy and America were at war), my aunt thought, So now what do I do? She did many things—among them, going to live in Hollywood and writing a best seller. She married Aldous Huxley, in his own right another example of resilience: victim as a young boy of a terrible eye disease that left him almost blind, he recovered and improved his eyesight by studying the use of the visual function and exercising the eyes with the Bates method, and so became one of the twentieth century's great writers.

Another example is Roberto Assagioli, founder of psychosynthesis. Assagioli was imprisoned by the fascist government in 1938 because he, a Jew, was organizing meditations on peace and internationalism. What could be more subversive? In prison he had an illumination: although he was prisoner, he could be inwardly free, and choose what attitude to take on in that, or any other, situation. Thus he planned a book titled *Freedom in Jail*. He was freed, but sometime after was forced to flee from Nazi persecution with his young son, to hide and to live day and night without shelter during the cold, damp winter in the Casentino region in Tuscany. Because of this, his son contracted tuberculosis and died a few years later. For a parent there is no greater loss. Nevertheless, Assagioli found the strength to carry on his life and work, teaching psychosynthesis, a system of psychology that contains, among its themes, the will and the capacity to handle the grave challenges of life and turn them into opportunities for growth. When I met Assagioli, who was then over eighty, he was a truly joyful man.

In telling these stories I realize I am speaking about people belonging to generations before mine, the one that gave rise to the baby boomers, born after the war. Subsequently, cradled in the consumer society, with an easier, more affluent life during peacetime, we became less resilient than the extraordinary generation that preceded ours. That generation had been tempered by war and recession. We have been less toughened, and our kids and grandkids likewise. It is now more likely for people to be upset by a cold, shaken by a parking fine, or miserable if they do not own the latest smartphone. The affluent society has perhaps rendered us a bit—or a lot—less resilient.

I would like to mention here also the quality of *hardiness*, often used as a synonym for resilience. I see a different shade of meaning. Resilience is the attitude of those who have experienced a difficulty and manage to emerge stronger than before. Hardiness is the quality of those who have yet to confront hardship, and so have the chance to get ready for it. Hardiness is the disposition to resist being intimidated by difficulties. We all know that life is a succession of challenges: from conception to birth through the infancy years, from the start of school, to adulthood, and from the first appearance of old age, to death. Like a wickedly inventive magician who is conjuring one unpleasant surprise after another, our life in each of its phases presents us with ever new hurdles.

To understand our degree of hardiness, we can try this thought experiment. We first ask ourselves what frightens us: cold or heat, toil, solitude or crowds, responsibility, work, discomfort, difficulty with others, sickness and death. Then we try to understand how we internally assess these predicaments. What emotions, what fantasies, arise in us when we think about them? What mental picture do we construct? We can then imagine a new attitude in relation to these future trials—a tougher stance, one that reframes the obstacles and lightens the difficulties. For example, if you have been offered a new job that is promising but difficult, you can think, It will be hard to wake up earlier in the morning to go to work, have more responsibility, be exposed to criticism, carry out tiring tasks, worry about the threat of failure. Or you can perceive it as an opportunity for developing new abilities. Another example: If you think about aging, you can see it as a brutal degeneration of your capacities, a ruthless reduction in physical strength, mental capacity, and economic level; a period of unhappiness and disintegration, which you face with a mixture of resignation and terror. Or you can perceive old age as a period in which to maintain as much as possible your psychophysical capacities, bring to fruition all you have learned, and develop a deeper awareness—perhaps wisdom.

Could it be that failure is actually an essential ingredient of human psychological development—and that people who are too protected actually risk becoming weaker? The psychologist Jonathan Haidt quotes a beautiful passage from the Chinese philosopher Meng Tzu: "When heaven is about to give someone a great responsibility, it will train his mind first with suffering, subject his nerves and bones to hard work, expose his body to hunger, make him poor, place obstacles on the way of his undertakings, to stimulate his mind, strengthen his nature, and improve him in areas where he is not yet competent."

The thesis of Haidt and others is that we need adversity to develop our strength to the maximum. In contrast to posttraumatic stress, he talks about posttraumatic *growth*. Clearly this is not a case of wishing misfortune and sickness upon anyone. However, we can tread the way of growth (as opposed to frozen immutability) only on the condition that we expose ourselves more to challenges and risks. Thus we are less protected and secure. It is in such situations that we draw on our greatest strength. This is particularly true during a critical period of our life: the formative years between fifteen and twenty-five years of age.

We know that certain elements favor resilience. Studies of resilience, made on individuals and populations that have endured misfortune and have picked themselves up again, describe various protective factors. First, solidarity: the comfort and nearness of others give strength and the capacity to start again. Second, self-esteem: if you believe you are competent, and if you are in touch with your qualities and resources, then you are more likely to make it. Third: a different reading of circumstances. The donkey in the story sees dirt showering onto him not as the weight that will bury him, but as the material that will help him climb back up. Fourth: a practical, future-oriented attitude and optimistic outlook. This means to concentrate on what needs to be done, with no regrets about the past. Fifth, self-control: we have already seen in a previous chapter how mastery helps us cope in the jungle of life. We could add the so-called healthy self-defense mechanisms, such as positive illusions (dreams that are not likely to be fulfilled, but are nevertheless a driving force), and, last but not least, a sense of humor.

What strikes me most about resilient people is their capacity not to be discouraged while facing unfavorable evidence; to consider defeat a distant possibility, and not an ineluctable destiny—and so to continue fighting even in the face of logic and common sense. There is the story of the two mice. They fell into liquid, and neither could swim. One was desperate and, believing his predicament was hopeless, gave up and drowned. The other kept flailing his legs, refusing to give up. After a while this mouse noticed that the liquid into which he had fallen was solidifying, which enabled him to reach the edge of the container: the cream had turned to butter.

And now we come to a philosophical question. Resilience is often seen as an example of adaptation: like the metal that returns to its former shape after being struck, the injured human being adapts to new circumstances and returns after the trauma to his or her former self. Here we can feel hovering a framework that has powerfully and consistently steered our thought, particularly during last century: the concept of homeostasis, the idea that our whole being is bent on the conservation of the preexisting state—with the corollary that our greatest aspiration is to regain and preserve equilibrium. This is evident at the physical level, where the various systems tend to oscillate in a range of minimum variations, in order to maintain the balance that supports life. The fasting blood glucose, for instance, should oscillate between 70 and 130 mg/liter. The homeostatic model has been applied to all our elementary needs. I am hungry, I eat. I am cold, I cover myself. I am sleepy, I sleep. And so forth. Obviously this is true at the physical level. But it is questionable whether the same criterion can be applied to *all* human predicaments—including our most passionate dreams, our bravest endeavors, our most thrilling encounters and projects. This could be the tyranny of reductionism. In this perspective our supreme happiness would be a regular and predictable existence. But is that really so? In truth, our life is an adventure: We want what we do not have, we endeavor to understand what we do not know, we seek sensations we have never felt before. We want to love more, and be creative. It is the *new* that interests us.

The homeostatic view of human existence is misleading, because it cancels any narrative. In fact, it regards each human act as an attempt to return to a condition of perennial, nondescript tranquillity. Our life would then be a series of deficits, followed by the attempts to eliminate those deficits. And that would be all.

Actually, we are what we are as a result of our ups and downs, our defeats, our various hurdles, even our illnesses. A series of events have molded us, have helped us understand and grow—they are not just stimuli that have disturbed a preexisting balance.

Seen this way, resilience is not merely adaptation. It is the way of strength. And resilient people who survive a misfortune do not remain the same. After the trauma, they do not only resume strength and return to their original way of functioning. They have grown stronger. They have a richer notion of their own powers. They have developed new faculties. They have seen a different dimension of life—and they are wiser. This is a whole lot more than mere adaptation.

There are two physical processes that can help us better understand resilience. One is tempering: steel, when subjected to high temperatures and then suddenly cooled, changes its internal crystalline structure, and is said to be *tempered*, that is, made stronger. A similar procedure is adopted in glassmaking, in which the glass is made to reach up to seven times its original strength. Another process is in the field of medicine. It is the vaccine: the introduction into our organism of the very bacteria to which we want to be immune. To deal with this controlled invasion, our immune system produces new antibodies; in the event of a real invasion, they will be able to defeat the same microbe. Thus the organism is reinforced. Both processes have been transferred into common parlance: "I am immune to such insults." "Adversity has tempered me." They are two examples of how an attack or a pressure, instead of weakening, ends up strengthening.

This is the school of life (sometimes called "the school of hard knocks"), which, in presenting us with difficulties that are apparently too tough for us to handle, actually tests us. Later we realize that those difficulties bring to light our hidden abilities, widen our mental outlook, and sometimes transform us. In my psychotherapy practice I have met all kinds of people who have been through terrible traumas: war, concentration camps, abandonment by parents, rape, loss of a child or partner, betrayal by friends, financial disaster, suicide of a dear one, forced emigration, hunger, poverty, drug abuse, prison, earthquakes, and other natural disasters. Some of them still needed to heal from those wounds; others mainly had to rediscover in themselves their own strength, their will to live and start over. In all of them I have seen, in varying degrees of liveliness and strength, and ready to rise again after the downfall, the indomitable resilience of the human spirit.

In the school of life we have much to learn. The learning process happens through our trials. Lucia, for instance, is going through the distressing breakup of a relationship in which she had invested all of herself. After a long period of seeing no way out of her suffering, she is beginning to think she can make it on her own, and to find her autonomy. Leonardo has had financial troubles, and realizes that previously he was living above his means, that his life was artificial. In the new and more modest lifestyle he has been forced into, he rediscovers the value of simplicity and genuine love. Giuseppe came close to death in a shocking car accident. It is this encounter with near death that helps him, after recovery, to distinguish between what is deceptively significant and what is truly fundamental. After facing death, everything became simpler and clearer.

Those who are not resilient see suffering and misfortune as defeat, or as an enigma with no solution. They perceive themselves as impotent, and the future as an infinite repetition of the present. Those who are resilient see adversity as an opportunity for transformation, themselves as competent to manage it, and the future as renewal. We have here different interpretations of life—what Martin Seligman, the founder of Positive Psychology, calls different "explanatory styles."

This different way of interpreting our life combines in the resilient with a determination and vigor that prevent resigning to defeat. For example, a longitudinal study over twelve years monitored 400 employees of Illinois Bell Telephone. The company had halved its workers through massive cuts, and the surviving staff had to endure abrupt changes in their tasks and responsibilities; many had also faced the risk of redundancy and the chaos of restructuring. Of these 400 people, two-thirds ended up with serious problems: heart attacks, strokes, obesity, depression, substance abuse, as well as poor work performance. One-third instead survived in a better than normal condition. The study tried to uncover what their secret trick had been. The researchers concluded that it was a question of a different attitude, summed up in three words: commitment, control, challenge. Instead of isolating themselves and withdrawing into their shells of depression and resignation, these people got busy, holding meetings and interacting with colleagues and bosses (commitment); they actively tried to influence the decisions made by the management, and to take hold of the reins (control); and they perceived the problems as opportunities for changing their lives for the better (challenge).

Another example. A study on resilience in sport looked in-depth at twelve Olympic gold medalists: eight men and four women. The researchers wanted to understand how life's difficulties had influenced their path toward triumph. They found that all these athletes had undergone stress: first of all, the normal stress of high-level competition, and then more specific difficulties—injuries, exclusion from the team, defeats, and personal experiences, such as illnesses and relationship problems. They also found that, according to the athletes, it was precisely these difficulties that had made them stronger and helped them win. The difficulties were essential in the process, because the subjects experienced them as tests, not as defeats or hindrances. Life had challenged and stretched them, so they brought out all their anger, trained with greater determination, and hungered for victory even more intensely.

Mircea Eliade points to this process of strengthening in the initiation into puberty found in various cultures all over the world. Children's maturation to adulthood involves an initiation with frightening and even cruel aspects. It represents the death of what has been. For Eliade, death in this sense is the possibility of regeneration and renewal. The alchemical process has the same principle: to obtain gold, you must go through decomposition. And several myths, which exist in all parts of the world, recount heroes eaten by a fish or a monster (as we saw in the chapter "Autonomy: Relying on Our Own Strengths"). It is the sojourn in the belly of that creature that symbolizes death and is at the same time an occasion for acquiring wisdom. Death is not the end, but a necessary passage to a new life.

This is what happens—or can happen—to someone who experiences a calamity. After a dark period, rebirth may not come straightaway. We have to go through a period of darkness and silent transformation. In psychotherapy these stages are well known. It is here that the metaphor of the resilient metal—which immediately resumes its shape after a blow—no longer fits. Often, for resilience to become manifest, a period of apparent immobility, suffering, and darkness is necessary—sometimes a long period. Nothing seems to happen except the pain, but meanwhile the seeds of future transformation are at work, and an unconscious elaboration is occurring and will reveal itself in rebirth.

The capacity to rise again is the mark of the phoenix, the Egyptian bird that burns and rises from its ashes. The principal myth of our civilization is the death and resurrection of Christ. Whatever theological sense we may give to this story, literal or symbolic, its meaning for all of us is clear: We may suffer, be torn and trampled upon, insulted, scorned, and abandoned. And we may descend into the deep darkness of death. But there we can indeed find the means to come back, stronger and more vital than ever.

Changing Perspective

Difficulties, problems, mishaps: we do not wish them on anyone. Yet, far more than ease and success, harsh and uncomfortable experiences can evoke in us resources that, in easier situations, may remain dormant. Here we shall see how it is possible to face hardship with a different attitude, and to transform it into a chance for learning and growth. In Italian we have a soccer expression: *cambiar gioco*—"to change one's play." It means suddenly sending the ball into a completely different part of the field, in order to surprise the adversary and start again in a new way. In the problematic circumstances of life, we can learn to change our play, too.

Remember always: The will is not just doing this or that. It is also consciously and deliberately changing our inner attitude.

Exercise

Think of a past hardship in which you summoned all your inner strength, your will, intelligence, and passion. From that experience, however hard, you emerged stronger, and perhaps wiser.

Now choose a current difficulty: a situation you would prefer did not exist—but does. With your eyes closed, observe all the reactions you have to it. What happens to your body when you think about it? How is your breathing? What are your posture and muscular tensions? What feelings does this problem arouse? Anger, dismay, despair? And with what strategies do you face it? You may find yourself dealing with this plight according to automatic reactions and superseded ideas—in other words, with blunted weapons.

Now think of the resources of strength and intelligence, will and love, resilience and energy, that this state of crisis can elicit in you. What new modality can you activate to face this difficulty? How can you change your play? Think it through in detail.

PRACTICAL HINTS

A basic mistake in this exercise is to confuse a difficulty with our way of handling it. The difficulty itself is one thing. Our way of handling it—with despair or confidence, resignation or energy, unconscious reactivity or purposeful imaginativeness—is quite another.

INTEGRITY

Inner Unity

Once upon a time there was a man who roamed the world in search of true justice.

What is right? What is wrong? He wanted a definitive answer. He traveled everywhere, without ever finding justice. The last place left for him to explore was a forest. There he found a little cottage. Through the windows he looked inside, and saw many candles burning. Curious, he entered, and noticed that the house was much bigger than it appeared from outside. Innumerable candles were arranged on long shelves. Some were burning strong and bright; others were weaker, and closer to extinction.

"What are you looking for? Can I help you?" asked an old man who had suddenly appeared at his side. "What are these candles?" asked the man. "They are the lives of each one of us. On the candleholder you can see somebody's name. When the candle burns out, that soul dies." "Which one is my soul's candle?" "Follow me." The old man led him through long tunnels full of candles. At last they reached his candle. Horrified, the man realized that it was near the end.

At that very moment another candle died out: it meant some-

one had just passed away! The man grew more anxious still. Soon he noticed that right near his candle was one much bigger and brighter, with plenty of wax left to burn. He looked around. The old man had disappeared. He realized he was alone. A thought came to him: Why not swap the brightly burning candle with his? He took hold of it, and was about to do the swap.

But right at that moment the old man reappeared beside him.

The old man asked him: "Is this the justice you are looking for?"

The words left him dumbfounded. The old man vanished, and then also the candles, the cottage, and finally the whole forest. The man remained there, meditating on justice—and on how easy it is to betray one's values. Or to forget one's own inner voice.

—HEBREW TRADITION IN AFGHANISTAN

Integrity means to respect our own values, and to act in harmony with them. We all have principles we believe in. Justice, love, protection of the weak, freedom, duty. Are they empty, grand words? To be sure, that is often the case. But no society would survive if these values were not at least partly respected. We hold them, or are unaware that we take them for granted. As we shall see, this happens, after a fashion, also in some animals. Values are a biological fact, not just an emotional event or a spiritual given.

Do we live in a world of honest and trustworthy souls? You know we do not. On the contrary, the highest values are betrayed every moment in favor of immediate advantage (like the man in the Afghan story, who was searching for justice and settled for survival), or because of social pressure, or inertia. But when this happens, we do feel something is wrong. Everyday dishonesty, on both the large and small scale, is before our eyes. Each day we see arrogance, injustice, selfishness. To speak of integrity may seem out of place. But I do not believe this is so, and now I shall explain why.

Working in psychotherapy, I am privileged to see what happens behind the scenes, so to speak. People's manifest, public behavior is at times malevolent and offensive, perhaps dishonest. But I get to explore at length what goes on in the inner world. I know that what may seem evident and straightforward from the outside is actually much more varied and multifaceted. I know there are ambivalences, doubts, torments, and conflicts. I also know values exist—principles to which each of us holds—ardently or halfheartedly, or maybe without even being realized. If we violate them, we feel uneasy, clearly upset, or more elusively troubled.

We can hide this discomfort from ourselves and others. We can make compromises, reformulations, rationalizations. But in so doing, we will feel cut off from a part of ourselves that can nourish us with strength and vitality. We will feel, perhaps darkly, that we have betrayed what we most believe in. And that is an unpleasant feeling. Something has gone wrong: and this thought will be unrelenting. For years, through my work, I have accompanied people in their inner explorations, and am sure that conscience exists. In some it is more clear and alive, a true guide.

In others it is stern, rigid, and obsessive: a dictator. In others still, it is dormant, but even then, when violated, it is capable of causing grief. You do not repress only sexuality and anger. You may also repress the voice of conscience.

Certainly complete coherence is impossible or undesirable. To contradict ourselves, make mistakes, change our mind, perhaps cheat: this is the stuff we humans are made of. But some people are coherent without being rigid. They have integrity without losing flexibility. This is similar to what Ronald and Mary Hulnik call "Loyalty to your Soul."

Imagine two compartments in your brain (or your soul, or psyche; choose the metaphor that works best). In one you have your values: what you believe in more than anything else; if those values did not exist, you would not be what you are; there would be no point in having relations with others, in making plans, in living. In the other compartment are your actions: what you concretely do in the world; everyday actions, such as brushing your teeth, crossing the road, throwing out the garbage, paying for parking, working. What is the distance between the two compartments? Do they communicate easily? Or does each lead its own existence, wholly cut off from the other? How much transparence and congruence are between them? Let us say, for example, that in the first compartment I uphold the importance of protecting the environment. But in the second, I dump garbage without bothering to recycle it, or throw away plastic bottles on the beach, or leave the motor running while the car is stationary—just to keep the air conditioning on. Or: I champion love and solidarity, but mistreat my wife, abuse my coworkers, and do not help a friend in need. In such cases I am leading two parallel and incompatible lives. And I will be weaker and divided, because my words and beliefs will have no power, and my daily actions will not be pervaded by the energy of strong thought and congruent emotion.

Integrity means to be at one with ourselves. What we think, what we feel, and how we behave become a coherent whole. In this way we feel that we experience ourselves as complete and present in what we do, say, and are. We carry the fortifying authority of inner consistency.

If this is not the case, we are ill at ease. If we see such incoherence in others, we feel distrust, disdain, or even disgust—especially if we trusted them in the first place. Think of people who cheat or steal; who change their minds according to personal advantage, or say one thing and do another; who are your friend only in fair weather, or just plainly break promises. All these people end up disappointing and infuriating us. Including the electrician who said he would come, and then does not show up.

The voice of conscience is free; it is given to us at no extra cost. But the moment we try to follow its requests—we are tested. That takes commitment, watchfulness, and will. Integrity often demands extra work or unpopularity. Respect your conscience, and you may be regarded as old-fashioned, stupid, or naive. Integrity comes at a price.

On the other hand, coherence between values and behavior gives us a feeling of strength.

Here are a few examples. Two people have a relationship; after some time they realize that what mattered to them (love, warmth, and sharing) has dropped to almost zero. The easier solution would be to ignore it and muddle along, living under the same roof, but with a pervasive sense of falsehood. The right and stronger one would be to separate. And that is what they do.

A husband is tempted to have an extramarital affair. The woman he is attracted to offers him passion, novelty, transgression: the wonderful promises of new love. It is an irresistible temptation—or nearly. But still, he loves his wife and has no intention of ruining their marriage. To start a secret relationship and pretend everything is normal, make up stories and excuses, devise plots in order not to be found out, invent a bunch of fail-safe plans—all of this violates the criterion of honesty and transparency he has always held dear. So he decides to say no.

A woman can get her hands on a small treasure, easily, quickly, and without risk: jewels that are part of a shared inheritance. She is the only one who knows. She could keep them for herself and not say a word. Instead, she tells her cousins and shares everything with them.

A shopkeeper realizes that a client he knows only by sight has given him too much money. With considerable effort, he tries to find him. He has to involve other people, ask questions, search far and wide, to look for a person for whom the only clues are physical appearance and make of car. He manages to find the client, and gives him back the money due.

A musician must perform a piece she knows well. She could

play it without much worry, giving the audience a faithful but unpolished performance. But instead she studies the whole piece anew and reinterprets it, with hard work that few would recognize. Thus her performance has greater depth and beauty.

A university professor finds facts that contradict his life's research. With great intellectual honesty he acknowledges not only the new evidence, but becomes chief critic of his own theses—the best method, in his opinion, for making them strong and true.

By now you are probably wondering if this chapter is a collection of moral exhortations. No such danger. My thoughts come from following people's inner stories, their choices, their defenses, their integrity. I know that scruples, feelings of guilt, conflicts between duty and pleasure, categorical imperatives, and a wish for justice are all part of the stuff we are made of, and are therefore legitimate subjects of study.

Where do our guiding values—whether submerged or evident—come from? Are they innate and infused by a divine source, and therefore the territory of religion and not psychology? Are they the result of cultural conditioning? Or are they a much older legacy—a series of adaptive behaviors that, in the long evolutionary struggle, have enabled us to survive? Survival for us humans meant not only to fight against one another, but above all to get along, mutually understand one another, and collaborate.

It is hard to give a straight answer to these questions. An excellent anthropological study on the feeling of justice was developed in fifteen different societies in several parts of the world, including Ghana, Papua New Guinea, Tanzania, Siberia, and Fiji. The researchers studied value differences in various kinds of societies. They put their subjects to the test by having them play games (cheating was possible), which measured their propensity for justice toward people they did not know, as well as their willingness to punish wrongdoing. They found that individuals in small groups who make their living by hunting and fishing, and therefore keep their catch for the small community they belong to, when it comes to strangers, do not care much about justice. On the other hand, those who subsist by buying food through wider commercial transactions, and who therefore belong to broader social groups, and follow monotheistic religions such as Christianity and Islam, behave according to inner rules of honesty and trustworthiness also with strangers; and they expect that their rights be respected in return. This study concentrated on equity toward strangers, not toward the people of the same group. The conclusion was that the sense of justice is not innate, but the result of social conditioning.

Other kinds of research reach very different conclusions. In a child psychology study, researchers showed forty-seven children, about fifteen months in age, a video in which an adult gave two other adults some biscuits and a glass of milk. But in some instances the sharing was not equal; one of the two received more biscuits and milk. The majority of children noticed the fact: it is a phenomenon called "violation of expectation" that can be detected in children's eye movements. If we expect things to go a certain way, and they go another way, we will be surprised and pay more attention. This is what happened with these children. They noticed when the sharing was not equal, and the experimenters recorded that reaction. It was their way of saying they expected the sharing to follow fairer rules.

In a subsequent experiment, the same children were given two toys, and then asked to choose the one they liked more. When an adult then asked a child: "May I play, too?," some offered their favorite toy, others the one they had discarded, and others none at all. Those who in the first experiment had had a more marked reaction to injustice were also the ones more disposed to share their favorite toy. Children—some more than others—have a sense of justice. But if you are a parent you already know this.

Another study showed that our brain appears to be made especially for distinguishing between justice and injustice. A group of subjects, who had already received thirty dollars, were given hats with balls inside—some containing nothing, others a bonus of fifty dollars. Meanwhile, their brains were monitored by brain imaging, to see which brain areas were most active. Particular focus was on the striatum and the prefrontal cortex—areas usually associated with evaluation. The brain showed a different reaction to equal and unequal distribution, showing a clear preference for the first. According to the researchers at Rutgers University, where the study was carried out, this indicates that our brain is naturally disposed to seek and create equality and equity. We have similar findings for truth telling: it is easier for our brains to tell the truth; if we lie, the brain, indeed our whole organism, must make much more effort. Truth comes more naturally to us.

So we can ask: is the capacity for moral judgment inherent in every human being? As Shaun Nichols points out in his book *Sentimental Rules*, we can better understand this point thanks to an important distinction: that between moral and conventional rules. Children are able to distinguish between a moral violation (hitting a classmate or stealing) and disobeying a rule (chewing gum in class, or daydreaming during math class). The first kind is considered much more serious, and can be generalized to other countries—in China you must not hit or steal—you refrain from doing it because it harms others and is wrong. The second kind of violation is seen as less important and not in itself unjust, but bound to other people's approval: if you want to be accepted, you have to obey a rule. The conventional violation can be questioned. A study on Amish students, for example, found that most students believed that if God were to make the rule that you could work on Sundays, then it would be all right to do so. The moral violation, instead, offends a deeply rooted intrinsic order: in the same study, the majority of Amish students (80 percent) maintained that if God were to permit hitting others, it would still be wrong to do so.

Do not think for a moment that humans are the only creatures who seek justice. The tendency also exists in the animal kingdom—at least in the more evolved species. Take the studies on capuchin monkeys. First they were trained to give back to the experimenters a granite stone within sixty seconds of the request. The restitution of the stone was rewarded with a cucumber. The researchers then repeated the same sequence with other monkeys, in the presence of the ones who had already participated in the experiment. The reward was again a cucumber, but at other times it was grapes (much more desirable), and sometimes the reward was free—that is, without the monkeys' having done anything to earn it. In short, the monkeys were confronted with a patently unjust situation. The reaction of the monkeys in face of unequal disadvantageous treatment was strong: they refused to participate in further experiments, or they refused to eat the cucumbers they were offered, or even showed anger toward the researchers.

In a study on rats done at the University of Chicago, the sense of justice takes the form of altruism. One rat was shut under a glass dome. Another rat nearby was free, and was given chocolate—a rat's favorite food. But the rats did not eat the chocolate while their mate was closed under the glass. First they freed him, then they shared the chocolate. Other rats, equally fair, but more cautious, first ate the chocolate, leaving half for the mate—whom they freed after eating their own portion.

From these studies a basic fact emerges: The sense of justice—or something resembling it—is active in human beings and other animals. In some it is more marked than in others, and is surely subject to cultural conditioning. In certain circumstances it is obscured or absent.

We may experience the sense of justice through an inner voice. Maybe we often forget it, or do not listen to it. But it exists. And more important, to forget to listen to it can cost us dearly. At the individual level, it means that our ethical signaling system is not working well, or we are not prepared to hear it. This inner deafness can cause us discomfort and reduce self-confidence. We do not feel whole anymore, or feel torn by conflict and try desperately not to heed a part of us we know is wiser and more just. If we take it to the social level, it becomes even more evident. Would you entrust our society to people incapable of feeling what is just, who are accustomed to privilege and who accept corruption?

Consider this experiment dealing with inner voice. The subjects had to press a button each time the word *go* appeared on the screen, and were not to press it when *no go* appeared, as fast as possible. The difficulty arose because the *no go* command was much less frequent, so it was easy to make mistakes. The task was made more complex by another factor: during the entire experiment the subjects continually had to silently say, "Computer, computer" (the idea was to interfere with their inner voice), or else they had to draw colored circles on paper. Whereas drawing did not influence the results, inner repetition of the word brought a higher number of mistakes. The goal of the experiment was to see what happens when we interfere with our inner voice by creating an artificial one. The upshot: the choices became more impulsive—and the mistakes increased. According to the experimenters, when we are confronted with crucial choices, it is wise to wait a little, deliberate, and listen to our inner voice, which they believe is one of the most important characteristics of the human species.

This is about listening to ourselves. Though we may be more

in contact with our inner voice, it does not mean we necessarily listen to it. Here we come to the hard part. I would like to tell you the story of Zita. Left alone with her children after a separation (her husband just vanished), she had many struggles, and thanks to her remarkable business ability, managed to attain a good living standard. When she came to me, however, Zita revealed several insecurities, and she realized that earning money was compensating for her solitude and the lack of a partner. But I intuited that this was not the true problem she wished to discuss. There was something more secret and riskier. After a time, when our alliance was strong enough, she disclosed her secret: Zita was a tax evader. She had never paid her taxes. She had managed very ably to remain hidden and to evade, but was living in constant fear of being found out. She was scared she would sooner or later find the auditors at her doorstep. Still more important, she did not feel at home in her own skin. But what was keeping her awake at night was the knowledge that what she was doing was wrong. She wanted to put it right. There were several false starts— because meanwhile life went on with its problems and tasks distracting her from this worry. At last Zita made up her mind: she had to settle the matter, and to this end she went to an office, where they drew up a plan of down payments to remedy her contravention. Zita had to call upon her resources of courage and integrity. It was an uncomfortable process, but the reward was big. She felt honest, and no longer had to pretend to herself, or stoop to making compromises with her conscience, or fear that her kids would one day find out. She had done away with a huge burden that had been tormenting and weighing down on her. Above all, Zita felt stronger, since the act cost her considerable moral effort: first she had to look at herself, then speak with me, then admit her wrong to the authorities, and finally fork over the money.

We are complex and contradictory beings. We are selfish and capable of the worst misdeeds. We are also clever at inventing excuses, and ever ready to forget uncomfortable alternatives. We are fragile and distracted. But we also have tendencies for justice and equity, which seem to be part of our biological organism— just like the need to drink, eat, and sleep. We need justice. Perhaps this is due to inborn empathy: if we commit a wrong, we can in some way sense or imagine the damage we inflict to others. But our yearning for justice is also due—this is my hypothesis—to a need for coherence and meaning, in the same way that our minds seek refuge from chaos and try to find coherent explanations for events and deeds. Coherence, however, comes at a price, as we have seen. A certain strength is needed to obtain it. And this strength, when cultivated, gives a sense of fulfillment and solidity that yielding to a momentary gratification cannot give.

The result of not listening to our inner voice may well be a sense of guilt. Sometimes the feeling of guilt is exaggerated and pathological: it can manifest in countless scruples, big and small, in great rigidity, in obsessions that make us lose sight of what really counts. For others, the sense of guilt is completely absent. They are a social danger, because they have no ethical code to live by. They have lost their compass.

The sense of guilt has its value and meaning. It is right and physiological that we feel uneasy if we have offended someone, cheated, harmed someone by lying, or broken a promise. If it were not so, we could not have social coexistence.

Just look at the newspapers: politicians who take bribes or make promises they do not fulfill, doctors who are careless or invent needless cures, athletes who take part in doping or fixing matches, executives who live on lies and corruption, large-scale investors who cause financial ruins for the masses, manufacturers who sell products that harm people's health. The more we hear of these circumstances, the greater our anger and mistrust of our society, the more painful our sense of dismay and disgust. We feel we are living in a sick society, and this state of disarray takes away value and meaning from our choices and the future—our own and that of our kids. At the same time we feel a strong need for transparency and honesty. The break between ethical code and behavior causes dejection and social disharmony: even before being a moral question, it is an elementary requirement for enabling people to live together.

Dante understood and depicted this full well. For him, as a Christian, confession was a way to free oneself from feelings of guilt. He shows it as a passage he must cross to get from Ante-Purgatory to true Purgatory, thus to continue his ascent toward the fullness of Heaven, which represents the state of grace. The passage consists in three stone steps. The first is white: we need courage to look inside ourselves without defenses or excuses, with clarity and truthfulness. In doing so we will be unpleasantly surprised at our own imperfections and faults, which is why the second step is gray and all broken. This represents our shock when we look inside ourselves. We have to face our dark self— and that is an irksome task. But now we are stronger, because we have been honest with ourselves. The third step is red: this is the vital energy that resumes its flow. After the third step Dante passes through the gate and must not, for any reason, turn around. Relieved from the burden of the past, he is free to head into the future. And so are we.

This process is not about just confession, but full honesty with oneself. It seems to me that Dante's metaphor should be of interest to all of us. The sense of guilt for our past actions or omissions weighs on us and must be somehow acknowledged. In psychotherapy we often face past traumas, since they can be a heavy and obstructing burden, even when traumas seem to have been forgotten. But we also have to confront the ill feeling of not listening to our inner voice. Violated integrity weighs just as much as past trauma. Only by healing it can we attain to the third step: the red one, the flow of life, the happiness of energy.

To all this we must add a further consideration. In these past decades we have seen a radical expansion in the image science holds of the human being. For a long time the prevailing view was that civilized society was only a compromise for the purpose of living together and surviving, but beneath the thin layer of civilization we are brutal, selfish beings, given to overcoming others for our own benefit, seeking pleasure at all costs. This idea was widely accepted and is still predominant, and often upheld or taken for granted by the media. More recently, however, thanks to new research in various scientific fields, a new, more complex image of the human being is taking shape. Surely, we are driven by selfish impulses and emotions. Yet we are also motivated by the wish for collaboration, the need to give and receive warmth, the vital necessity to interact with other human beings and to belong to a community, and the desire to be useful and serve others. Also, we now know that we can gain a better state of health and inner balance from pro-social attitudes and behaviors, and they contribute to a richer and more composite image of who we are. It may be a less one-sided picture, since doubtless we are also cruel, selfish, territorial, and non-caring. But this is how we are made—we are an astonishing mix of conflicting traits.

The study of child behavior has also contributed relevant ideas on this subject. The image of the child has changed radically. Children are no longer seen as purely selfish, but as individuals capable of disinterested acts, spontaneous tenderness and solidarity, and behaviors marked by sociableness and collaboration. It would suffice to mention the observation of kindergarten children's behavior: When not guided, they show spontaneous friendly interactions, mutual help, and collaboration much more often than they show acts of bullying and power play. It is a very different image from the one portrayed in *Lord of the Flies* by William Golding. There, a group of schoolboys who have survived an airplane crash and are stranded on an island end up fighting a pitiless war among themselves. In reality children do not behave this way at all.

The study of altruistic behavior reveals that much of it is spontaneous and dictated simply by the desire to help others. For example, why is it that during the German occupation of France in the Second World War, many ordinary citizens decided to help Jews by hiding them, themselves running a serious risk? Why do so many people donate blood or bone marrow? Why are millions of people involved in volunteer work, giving their time and energy for the well-being of others? The answer turns out to be: because that is how we are made.

Research on the immune system, more precise and impersonal, can also clarify our ideas on this subject. Until the '80s it was thought that the immune system was not affected by our emotions and behavior. Research findings have shown this to be untrue. The immune system reacts to various vicissitudes in our life. We now know that stress lowers immune function. We also know that the immune system reacts favorably to pro-social behavior. Altruistic people have a stronger immune system. The same goes for endorphins, opioid substances secreted by our pituitary glands to generate pleasure: an act of kindness produces plenty of them. As a matter of fact, all the variables with which we measure a human being's psychophysical health are in favor of pro-social behavior. Altruists live longer, go to the doctor and psychotherapist less often, and are happier. Ultimately, this means we are organisms made for solidarity, tenderness, and collaboration.

Two other great phenomena come under the umbrella of pro-social behavior: forgiveness and the sense of belonging. In 2006 a conference of the American Psychological Association showed that the lack of forgiveness was a major health problem. People who carry in themselves a mass of unresolved conflicts and still active resentments suffer poorer health: lack of forgiveness is a measurable reality and must be regarded as a health cost. We must forgive others not in order to condone injustices, but to be well. Of particular importance is big, unresolved, and still active rancor among conflicting communities such as Israelis and Palestinians in the Middle East, or Catholic and Protestants in Northern Ireland, or Christians and Muslims in the Balkans: enmities perpetuated through generations.

The sense of belonging is also an aspect of pro-social emotions. It means to feel the support of others and be ready to offer it, thus enabling us to feel part of a whole, more protected and secure. To be in a community of people with whom we can talk, where we can lend a hand, where we can keep one another company, and on whom we can rely in case of need is fundamentally important for our physical and psychological well-being. To feel alone and isolated, without anyone in the world to communicate with, is a terrifying condition. And it is a time bomb for our health. Many are at risk, especially the elderly.

Why have I digressed into pro-social emotions and behavior? It is because in this book we are talking about inner strength and the will. This strength—this will, the capacity to persevere, master oneself, reach a goal—can be used for purely selfish purposes, and even destructively.

A strong will alone can do damage. In a fight for power, an

unscrupulous executive succeeds in eliminating another and excluding him from the control room; in a corporation, a board member deliberately spreads poisonous rumors about another member to destroy his reputation and get ahead; a newcomer to a business befriends a colleague in order to use his support and knowledge, then cynically drops him after getting what he wanted; an ambitious parent yells and plots to gain advantage for his son at soccer school. Or even more simply: someone pushes ahead in a line, elbowing his way, heedless of protests. Yes, our will may or may not be ethical. If it is not, we negate a part of ourselves that actually longs for friendship and human warmth. And if there is a schism between this deep aspect of our being and our habitual attitudes and behaviors, we will feel torn. In the short run we may believe we are stronger. But in the long run we will turn out to be weaker.

The dichotomy between altruism and egoism is, in reality, illusory. The best way to be well is to take care of others, interact with them, listen, and offer the best we can of ourselves, to be open and to love. If our will is aligned with these demands, we will feel well. This is integrity. If our will is in conflict, and serves only our selfish interests if not our destructive tendencies, then a dangerous divorce, perhaps disintegration, is at play.

Even criminals have a code of behavior—it is in their best interests. A Taoist story, steeped in the paradoxical humor of that tradition, tells of a man who asks the bandit Chih if robbers cultivate wisdom and morality. He replies: "To be sure, they do. To find oneself in a strange house and guess unerringly where its treasures are hidden, this surely requires inspiration. To be the first to enter needs courage; to be the last to leave requires a sense of duty. Never to attempt the impossible needs wisdom. To divide the spoils fairly needs goodness." And that is what it takes to become a respectable criminal.

The Guiding Star

Which criteria govern our decisions? What principles rule our life—and therefore determine how we relate to others, how we behave day by day? Usually it is a jumble of factors: impulses and wishes, dreams and hopes, fears and aversions; but also pressure from others, and who knows how many other factors of which we are not aware. Often there is conflict and confusion. It is like a rambunctious committee, with everyone fighting for the upper hand.

Sometimes principles, values, or qualities (whatever we call them) enter into play: justice, freedom, beauty, truth, love, health. In some cases these principles rule our life and give it coherence, meaning, and dignity.

In the following exercise we work on a hypothesis: what is, or could be, the principle you would like to guide and inspire you. Would you like a reference point in your life, a guiding star to show your path? Or do you prefer to just take what happens and let life run its course (this, too, may be a choice)?

Our values are often unconscious: they guide us without our knowing it. Or they come up in dramatic moments, or when we face crucial choices. To make them more explicit means to make them stronger.

Exercise

Think of what your guiding star might be—the value you most want to honor: truth, love, beauty, justice, etc. Remember that for now this is just a hypothesis, and that you can change it at any time.

Reflect for a few minutes on how your life would be if it were pervaded and guided by this principle.

With eyes closed, allow a symbolic image to emerge that represents for you this quality or principle. Then continue visualizing it for a few moments. Do not choose this image with your head: let it arise within you spontaneously. If the first image that comes is not convincing, wait for another one.

Symbolic images are alive. They have a wisdom of their own. You can imagine conducting a real dialogue with them. Inner thoughts and images have an independent life—what Jung calls "the reality of the soul" (*die Wirklichkeit der Seele*).

The quality chosen can give us answers to our doubts, point the way for us, enlighten us on a predicament. That image may put us in touch with the most insightful part of us, which we often just relegate to the unconscious.

Let the image disappear, and, for just a few moments, perceive your quality as an atmosphere or a living presence that can permeate and regenerate you. Breathe deeply and slowly. Each time you breathe out, imagine breathing that quality into the world around you.

PRACTICAL HINTS

Integrity does not mean fundamentalism. Letting a principle govern our life gives us a feeling of order and coherence. We need the will to reconnect us with that principle. It is like deciding the wavelength we want to tune into. This makes us feel freer. No coercion is needed. When there is compulsion of any kind, we are on the wrong path. In that case it is better to give it a miss and take the day off.

COURAGE

Challenging Fear

Two men, one rich and one poor, made a bet: "If you spend the whole night swimming in the sea alone, I will give you my cattle," said the rich man, who was also very greedy, "but if you do not succeed, you must give me everything you own." He was sure he would win: How could that man of few resources withstand a dark sea on a moonless night, in cold water, all alone? It was terrifying. He could not possibly do it.

The poor man accepted the bet. But then he began to worry. He was afraid he would die from cold, or drown, with no one to come to his rescue. Or, if he gave up, he would lose the little he had. He started thinking that accepting the bet was a mistake. He went to an old woman for advice. "Tell one of your relatives to build a fire on the shore," said the old woman, "and to keep it burning all night. While swimming in the sea, keep your eyes on the fire. It will warm you, even though it is far. It will give you the courage you need."

The man followed her directions. The waves roared. The cold chilled him to the bone. He was alone with himself. On shore, the guards of the rich man watched to see if he returned to dry land.

But he kept his eyes on the point of light far away, and it gave him the strength to carry on.

When dawn came, he knew he had won.

But the rich man did not accept it: "You have cheated! The fire reassured and warmed you. You should not have looked at it! I will not give you my cattle!"

So they went to a judge. This man also said the poor man had not won the bet. But the poor man did not give up. Finally they decided to take counsel from a man they both regarded as wise. His name was Abunawas, and he was also endowed with a good sense of humor. After listening to them, he did not make any comment straightaway, but instead invited the adversaries and their families to a large banquet the next day. All the guests arrived early, and stood outside to wait. Meanwhile enticing aromas issued from Abunawas's house. Soon the food was placed on display on the verandah, so all could see it. But it was not offered. Everyone's mouth was watering, yet the stomachs stayed empty.

Finally, after many hours, Abunawas came out and told everybody: "Now you can go." "What? No food?" The guests protested. "You smelled the aroma, is that not enough for you?" "The aroma by itself does not satisfy our hunger!" "You saw the food, did it not satisfy you?" "To see it does not count. We want to eat." "And so," said the wise man, "how can a faraway fire in the night warm a man swimming alone in the cold sea?"

And then, they all understood.

—ETHIOPIAN STORY

Some time ago I was in one of those huge underground parking garages. While I was walking back to my car, a woman approached me. She was in a state of alarm. "Help! Help! I cannot find my car. I am scared I will never get out of here!" She was panting and her eyes were open wide, as if she were having a panic attack. I told her I would help her find her car. We looked about, and I asked a few questions so as to figure out where it might be. I told her it was natural to be frightened in such an enormous and anonymous non-place. Gradually she calmed down. After a while we found the car. The woman cheered up, and then thanked me: "You are really smart. You should work as a psychologist!"

That woman was right to be afraid. I did not tell her, but deep down I, too, was pretty uneasy in that monstrous environment. The truth is, we are surrounded by a number of terrifying situations—both near and far. As I write, it is eight thirty in the morning. In coming to my study, I have listened to the news on the radio, bought the newspaper and glanced at the headlines. I hear that the euro, currency of 500 million people, is in danger (my own economic survival is at risk); the drought is worsening; a serious water shortage looms in the future; and food scarcities are predicted (my physical survival is uncertain). Unemployment is increasing, shops and businesses are closing (my sons' future is in danger). I hear stories of corruption and robberies, and horrendous crimes (civil society is disintegrating). Today there is also talk about the danger of an earthquake (the earth is trembling under my feet). It seems there is a new epidemic in the offing, the lethal virus is at our front door (I glimpse the end). On top of that, cosmic radiation is increasing (that is all we need).

Therefore, if we are missing out on the essential quality of courage, every aspect of our life suffers. In this chapter we will study the meaning and benefits of courage, and will see how this fundamental resource can be developed.

Every day we are subject to concentric attacks to our safety. It is no wonder then that, like the woman in the parking lot, we have panic attacks. It is as if we are all trembling inside. Doubtless, humanity has experienced all kinds of danger and catastrophe, and we hear their echo in our collective unconscious. Now it is different, however, because large-scale dangers are continuously fed to us in big doses as information items, and they invade our inner world with devastating energy. They are imagined dangers, yet they are huge.

In contrast, we have far fewer chances for putting ourselves to the test in perilous situations. Our Paleolithic ancestors had to risk perpetually. In hunting and gathering they faced fierce animals and difficult terrain. In mating, obedient to the incest taboo, they had to seek mates among foreign groups who were often hostile. Their very subsistence was exhausting and precarious. Survivors in that era were equipped to handle many a danger. We are their descendants. This appears to be the reason why many of us experience pleasure and a surge of energy in situations of risk, such as mountaineering, scuba diving, and parachuting (not me).

But risk is not just thrill seeking: it is also mastering fear. Two souls dwell within us: one ready to risk, because from this attitude come countless benefits; and the other fearful and protective. Which one will prevail?

This duality is well illustrated in an experiment conducted by Uri Nili in the Department of Neurobiology at the Weizmann Institute of Science in Israel. The subjects were in one of two categories. The first was of individuals who abhorred reptiles, and the other of people who had familiarity with snakes and were not afraid to handle them—the control group. The setting was most bizarre: the subjects were closed in an apparatus that permitted moment-to-moment visualization of their brains (magnetic resonance); behind their heads, a tape moved a live corn snake, attached with Velcro, closer or farther from them. Through a mirror, the subjects could see the snake behind them. By pressing one button, they could also bring it closer, or, if afraid, by pressing another button, they could move it away (the snake was not harmed). In order to study the different reactions, the experimenters sometimes used a toy snake instead of the real one, in which case all was much calmer. From this experiment they could see that two distinct parts of the brain came into play, depending on which button was pressed. If the subject was scared and made the snake move away, the amygdala was active—this is the cerebral area responsible for, among other functions, emitting alarm signals and generating fear. If instead the subject decided to bring the snake closer, this activated the subgenual anterior cingulate cortex (SGCC), a more recently evolved part of the brain associated with the executive function. In short, when we decide whether to risk or not, we bring into play our evolutionary history and our biophysical makeup: we can retreat and protect ourselves, or we can master our fear and come forward. Two parts of the brain and two different eras of our evolution come into play and confront each other. One becomes dominant.

In our everyday life, it is rare to come up against snakes. But many other dangers arise all the time: our physical, emotional, intellectual, and social limitations are shaped by the risks we do not feel ready to take on. Like strict borderlines, they define the area within which we live, and thus determine the kind of existence we create for ourselves.

Perhaps the best way to be clear about our borders is to examine our regrets. Think about the time you might have started talking with that attractive woman (or man) on the plane, but, because you were shy, you did not dare. And what about the important meeting in which you might have come up with an original idea—and then someone else spoke and took all the credit. Or perhaps there was a wonderful excursion that you thought was too demanding and adventurous, so you did not go. Or, because you underrated yourself, you gave up the offer of your dreams and settled for a more secure job. These are all examples of opportunities missed because of excessive caution.

When we wallow in regret, we suffer greatly. In small quantities, however, regret has a self-corrective function: it may offer useful information about our errors and limitations. Regrets are fairly precise indicators of risks we have chosen not to take because of fear or inertia. Every move we make can bring risks. We risk our physical well-being, we risk wasting time and money, not achieving anything, being rejected and embarrassed, making a bad mistake, or just being taken for a fool. So we do not step forward.

This caution means living each day in an atmosphere of dread and alarm. Our society contributes to this predicament by fueling our fears and profiting from them. Thus, we drive huge, tanklike SUVs; close our doors with ultrasafe locks; and insure ourselves against earthquakes, fire, burglary, illness, accident. We do not speak to strangers because the world is full of delinquents. We install fire alarms, burglar alarms, have medical checkups, put money aside for old age, stay connected so we do not feel lonely, remember scores of passwords to erect digital safety firewalls, and put a webcam everywhere to keep an eye on our personal safety.

If it is true that Greek mythology contains all the possibilities of the human mind and all its most important pathologies, then the sword of Damocles is an accurate metaphor for the ever-present fear of what may happen. Damocles was forced to sleep under a sword precariously hanging by a fine thread that could break at any moment, letting the sword drop and cut him open. Not the best recipe for sound sleep. This is the perfect scenario of the anxious: the feeling of ongoing alarm in which one constantly awaits a looming disaster that may never happen.

If you study the concept of risk you will find, both on the Web and by listening to people talk, that it is usually understood as a calamity to be prevented: The risk of a terrorist attack, for instance. Young people are at risk of drugs. The risk of bankruptcy. The danger of fire. And so on. Very few think that risk may be a basic element of growth and personal renewal. Yet it is.

There are several kinds of risk. First there is physical risk, in which you jeopardize your personal safety. Clearly, endangering your own or another's life in a foolish and unprepared way is a reckless and childish act. But it is also true that many sporting activities, such as mountain climbing or scuba diving or white-water kayaking, can bring about a profound transformation that does not happen to those who just sit in an armchair. These activities necessitate a trust in one's own capabilities, a watchfulness and a stretching of limits. We know we are moments away from possible death, and it takes paying attention to stay safe. Sporting activities with an element of risk increase self-confidence and put in perspective our everyday troubles.

Emotional risk is about moving beyond our comfort zone into areas of our inner being that are scary and embarrassing. It means opening to another person, risking exposure and ridicule; putting ourselves in situations in which we feel vulnerable. It also means letting others know parts of us we are perhaps reluctant to admit even to ourselves; for example, showing we are moved, speaking of our fears or sexual fantasies, admitting our weaknesses and limitations. We risk being made fun of, or blamed, or judged. And worst of all, we may be rejected.

And then there is social risk: to express publicly how we feel and what we believe in, even if it does not comply with the norm.

It includes dressing as we like, not as others say we ought; reading what interests us, not the latest best seller; filtering the banalities everybody is saying; listening to music that inspires us, not just the top ten. It also means befriending people outside of our social circle, profession, and shared tastes. Let us not forget that eccentrics, as a well-documented study shows, enjoy above-average health, just because they do not undergo the stress of being other than what they are.

Social belonging, as we have seen in a preceding chapter, has high biological and psychological value. To be part of a group is our evolutionary destiny: we cannot survive on our own. But sometimes the price demanded is too high. This happens when we are asked to renounce what defines us most. In some teenage circles, you are either in or out. To be excluded is terrifying. And to belong, one has to dress like the others, have the same interests, use the same words, hang out in the same places. Clearly, adolescents show this in an extreme and theatrical way, but conformism is present in all age groups. Sometimes the only way to feel well is to rebel. It seems a risk, but the real risk is the opposite: to conform, and become a walking mummy.

Intellectual risk is analogous. It means to adopt unfamiliar ways of thinking—or at least explore them. To look at the world from other points of view, instead of being shut in our own prejudices. It means also to have the intellectual honesty to say what we think without fear of making a blunder. To ask uncomfortable questions and allow ourselves to be wrong. And, when we are wrong, to have the sincerity and strength to acknowledge it. It is also the risk of stepping outside our own cultural confines, exposing ourselves to art forms and ideas that are alien to us: music, literature, and paintings that, far from blandly reassuring us, shake and shock us.

And then, as a synthesis of all kinds of courage, as the culmination of inner strength, we have the courage to be authentic. The concept of authenticity is commonly used for paintings, watches, and clothes: the original is always the best. "Authentic" means the true and excellent. The imitation is usually by a cheat. People, too, can be authentic or inauthentic. If they are inauthentic, they lose themselves, and betray falsity, unease, and hypocrisy. If they are authentic, they have the force of truth on their side; they have freshness, life, and spontaneity. It is the difference between a plastic flower and a real one. No one can say concretely how authenticity manifests, because each one of us expresses it differently. Certainly, the authentic know what they believe in and what they like; they are able *to be what they are*. And this is a strength. There are no precise indicators of authenticity, but all can recognize it when they see it. Being authentic requires courage, because the authentic are not always liked and accepted. True, the inauthentic may live at times a more comfortable and less demanding life. But we know, too, that in the long run inauthenticity leads to dissatisfaction and restlessness, at times also depression.

Risk is inherent in human existence. In all myths representing the conquest of self, the hero faces dangers and difficulties, and this ordeal transforms him or her into a new being, endowed with new knowledge and powers. Consider the example of Psyche as told in the story *The Golden Ass* by Apuleius. She is an inexperienced girl who has come to know and love the young god Eros. He responds at first, and then, when he is seen for what he truly is, runs away and disappears. Psyche has to find him again. To do so she is subjected by Venus (mother of Eros) to a series of terrible trials. She must sort out a huge pile of various grains and lentils in an absurdly short time. With the help of benevolent ants, she succeeds. Then she has to face fierce and dangerous rams and remove their golden fleece. For her third test she must climb to the source of the river Styx, which is protected by frightening monsters, and there she must fill a vessel with its pure water and take it back to Venus.

As the adventure proceeds, the tasks become harder and more dangerous. Psyche (who, as her name implies, stands for the human soul) must accept the challenge to face the fear and anguish of not succeeding, the feeling of being alone and inadequate to the arduous task. Luckily, as in all fables, helpers are forthcoming: they represent the inner resources we do not know we have. Psyche's fourth and last task is to descend to hell and meet the terrifying powers of the dark world to find a beauty cream for Venus. This is the hardest assignment, because it amounts to facing death. It is a task we will all sooner or later meet: reckoning with failure, emotional death, abandonment, utter defeat, error, the fall of our reference points, the failure to fulfill our hopes and most cherished beliefs, disintegration. Only thus can we find ourselves again. Psyche will succeed in this last venture, as long as she does not fall prey to curiosity and open the jar of beauty cream. But this is exactly what happens; the jar actually contains a magical perfume that puts her to sleep. This is the ultimate trap. Even though the mistakes are grave, a few are permitted on condition that Psyche have the courage to risk. In the end, Eros comes and saves her.

Like many other heroes or heroines, Psyche, in order to find the one she loves most, must face her worst fear. Risk is a multiplier of possibilities. Many risks, many possibilities. Few risks, few possibilities. No risk equals death. Paradoxically, to never take risks—to give in to our fears, never leave home, refuse new ideas, steer clear of new and unfamiliar people, spurn new challenges, never accept any tests—is a protective shield that puts us in a state of imaginary security. But it means the atrophy of all our functions, in other words, death—precisely what we were trying to avoid in the first place.

Instead, to have the courage to risk brings immeasurable benefits. First, it changes our basic attitude toward life. We would all like a safe and painless life, of course. We would like our respectability to be secure, our comfort never challenged. It is human to wish perfect security, but we know too well it does not exist. And if we do not step forward and find risk, in any event, risk will come and find us. Sooner or later insecurity comes, even if we are well protected. There is no absolute protection. If instead we do risk, our basic attitude changes. It becomes more flexible, readier for change; we understand that we will never really have all securities, and that sometimes we just have to bet.

After all, we ourselves are born of a bet: one sperm cell out of millions set off on a journey that for us proportionally equaled a trip to the moon, in a difficult, hostile environment. The probability of making it: one in 300 million. And once it arrived at its destination, the dangers were not yet over—on the contrary. But in the end we made it, and here we are.

Sure, we would like a comfortable life: this is a totally legitimate wish. We do indeed seek pleasure and try to avoid pain. This attitude shapes all aspects of our material life. We want escalators to do the climbing for us. We want houses and clothes to keep us warm, air conditioning to keep us cool. We want to sleep on soft beds, eat all kinds of refined food—and find it in the local supermarket. We want to move from place to place effortlessly. We delegate jobs to machines and automation. And meanwhile we expect endless pleasure and entertainment.

We have created an illusory world. Shielded by this protection, we try to forget that life is a battle demanding effort, attention, will, and courage. At every step we find snares, dangers, and trials. Difficulty is inherent in the very structure of our existence. Courage is the quality that best serves our survival.

Courage and risk help us take ourselves a little less seriously. If we make a fool of ourselves, so what? If we are ridiculed, it is not the end of the world. If we lose some money, we will not be ruined. If we are rejected, we can try once more in the future. If we fall down, we get up again. Otherwise we become like those children who cannot bear to lose. They play at checkers or ball or hide-and-seek, and when they lose, they throw a tantrum, cry and scream, because they experience a tiny defeat as a catastrophe, an annihilation—an evil to be avoided at all costs. This is a fairly common and understandable childish attitude—in a child. But as we grow, the fear of looking bad or failing stays with some of us as an unredeemed remnant from childhood. It is the terror of shame without remedy. But no! Risk helps us take it all in our stride—an often useful attitude to have.

We can understand several crucial aspects of courage from studies done on bomb-disposal experts, parachutists, and firemen. These people regularly risk their lives. Naturally they have fear. But fear can be gradually vanquished by three means: group support, the presence and solidarity of others exposed to the same dangers; technical know-how, the reassurance given by one's own competence; and finally familiarity with danger: day after day, facing a risky situation will slowly turn danger into a friend. The splendid quality of courage can be learned.

To openly confront the risks life brings us, without hiding from them, helps us strengthen our will and thus our psychic voltage. The path of least resistance is to avoid all risk and confrontation. Stay home and keep warm. Watch a movie on TV while eating chocolate. Keep a low profile. To face any risk, instead, entails a measure of friction with our lazy or apprehensive self. It takes will, and each time we use the will, we grow stronger.

To be brave enough to risk draws from our depth's unknown potentialities. We could envisage a pedagogy of risk, which consists in placing individuals in predicaments where the urgency and immediacy of the present situation forces them to learn. In a Zen story, an adept robber wishes to teach his son the tricks of the trade. He takes him along when he goes to rob a rich mansion. Once inside, in the innermost part of the mansion, he himself sets off the alarm and flees. The son is taken by surprise, then invents various strategies to trick those who come after him, and manages to escape. Obviously, he is upset with his father: "Why did you put me in danger?" The father asks him how he dealt with his ordeal, and the son relates all the tricks he thought up on the spot to escape. At the end the father smiles and says, "Nice work. You are learning."

As we take risks, whole new worlds reveal themselves to us. If you are scared of speaking in public and you decide to do it, you may discover that you have a talent for communication and an ability for teaching and self-expression. If you do not disclose your feelings, you may not enter the stupendous world of love— all love stories start by crossing the threshold of intimacy. That is the moment of risk and of mystery, when you cross a line knowing you cannot go back.

In confronting risk we discover that courage is one of the highest spiritual qualities. It has been said that courage is the basic quality, because it makes possible all the others. It is no coincidence that the Latin word for soul—*anima*—also means "courage," as a quality that is of the same substance as our being.

Courage has an element of nobility. In its highest aspect, it acts in defense of people or principles. The Carnegie Hero Fund in the United States has already rewarded (choosing from countless recommendations and 80,000 nominations) more than 9,000 people who have risked their lives in an extreme way (sometimes they died or were left maimed) to save another human being. The rescuers met different dangers: fire, drowning, an oncoming train, electric shock, shark attack, armed assault, and others. The statute of the foundation requires that the rewarded not be professionals (firemen or police), and not relatives of people saved, but complete strangers. They are people who suddenly and spontaneously helped someone in grave difficulty, at risk to their lives. And they did just that—throwing into doubt all we have heard about the selfishness of human nature.

These were extreme cases, and many of us will never have to face such an event. But we all meet situations in which we can exercise courage, and each time we do, we will come out stronger and more confident. As for the man in the tale at the beginning of this chapter, it helps, in the dark, cold night, to watch, even from afar, a burning fire: it helps to have a point of reference, a beacon that shines for us, and warms and comforts us. In this way, as the tale goes, we do not cheat. This is not an aid from outside. Success comes from the will to keep in touch with a worthwhile purpose. Otherwise, life does indeed become a cold, dark night. And the burning fire can be many things for us. We can face dangers if we know we are doing it for a good reason: love for someone, a goal, an ideal, and even earning money or advancing in our career or some other crucial development in our life.

I think of my clients who had excessive reactions to everyday commitments: Ciro, who had to give PowerPoint presentations to a group of executives in the firm, and could not bear all eyes on him; Eleonora, who broke out in a cold sweat before exams, even though she had studied; Ester, who was scared of the freeway; Michele, who was dumbstruck in the presence of a bullying neighbor; Giorgio, who was afraid to be alone; and Mariasole, who could not stand anonymous crowds. All of them managed, for better or worse, on and off, to be braver and face up to critical situations. They did it by learning to breathe (after all, *animus* is also "air," the breath), by finding their center, by visualizing themselves as serene when confronting the challenge, and by approaching difficult situations gradually (when possible), thereby slowly increasing their inner strength.

Courage is an affirmation of life. Fear of death paralyzes us. Will we let it win? Then we will come to a standstill. Do we really want to go through life like that? If we risk, if we forge ahead and affirm ourselves, we feel a surge of energy. It is the energy of the new. Courage shuffles all the cards. Inevitably risk brings change, and with it spiritual regeneration.

In many cases, someone's courage changes not only her own life, but that of others. Moral or civil courage is to affirm our position at the risk of our own safety in the face of injustice or dishonesty. It means intervening, for instance, when a weak person is a victim of bullying. While others look away and do nothing or hurry on, the brave will make themselves heard. If everyone keeps quiet, no good can come of it. As the Irish philosopher Edmund Burke said: "All that is necessary for evil to triumph is that good people do nothing."

At times an act of bravery has huge and unimaginable benefits. I think of the story of Rosa Parks, the African American woman from Birmingham, Alabama. One day she was going to work on the bus as usual. At the time segregation was still in force. Blacks like her had to sit in a separate part of the bus. She was seated there. But on many buses, the white area was expanded and the black area reduced, as had happened on that day. The conductor ordered her and three other passengers to move from their seats and leave them to white passengers. The three obeyed, but she did not. She was tired of suffering injustice. Right then she decided to resist. Later she wrote that the determination she felt at that moment pervaded her body like a warm blanket in the winter. The police arrested her. But the next day thousands of blacks out of solidarity started not to use public transport. A benevolent force was set in motion: the peaceful protest that was soon to become part of civil rights history had begun.

In exceptional cases like this one, a single act of courage changes a whole era.

Evoking Courage

You can develop courage (or any other quality) with the help of the creative imagination. Visualization evokes states of mind, thoughts, and actions, and therefore generates the corresponding brain circuits. If we imagine being brave, we become brave, but only if we repeat the visualization a number of times, so as to assimilate it fully. This is the deliberate and conscious creation of a new way of being.

Exercise

With your eyes closed, take a few slow, deep breaths. In your own way, imagine being brave. Imagine the state of mind of one who is not intimidated by difficulty or threat. Imagine the determination inherent in courage. Feel also the emotion of courage—an emotion of the heart.

How does a brave person think? Imagine thinking in that way. A brave person is ready to bet, thinks about the opportunities she is opening for herself and for others with her courage. Her thinking is open.

Imagine feeling the dynamic boost of courage. In the laboratory of the imagination, give yourself permission to think, do, and say all that is usually outside your scope in real life. Imagine feeling courage as inner strength. You are not intimidated by any threat or obstacle. You experience courage as pervading every cell of your being.

Exit your comfort zone. Imagine daring: not reckless or dangerous acts, but reasonable and constructive risks. New initiatives, new attitudes, new relationships. Imagine all this vividly, and in as much detail as possible.

PRACTICAL HINTS

This exercise is an example of will used intelligently. Instead of forcing yourself to be brave, instead of trying not to be fearful, imagine that you are *already being courageous*. It is much easier and more efficacious.

Some say it is impossible to imagine themselves being brave. But it is not so. In the imagination everything is possible—you can imagine being six feet tall, or being able to fly, or having a nose like Pinocchio's. You can also imagine being brave. It may seem a little strange at first, but you can.

And remember, this is not a daydream. It is the inner creation of a new way of being. It is quite different from letting yourself go in fantasy: "Wouldn't it be wonderful if . . ." Rather, you form a clear and precise idea of how you would like to become.

THE STATE OF GRACE

What Gives Meaning to Our Life

Once upon a time a young woman became mortally ill. She grew worse every day. Several doctors had tried to cure her, but no one succeeded. Her husband was desperate. Finally he went to a wise healer, who smiled reassuringly and said it could be done. He told the husband the optimum astral conjunction for his cure to be applied. Then he said: "This is what you have to do: Find a skull. Then go to the desert, and when it rains, position it so that it collects water in its cavity. At some point a frog will jump over the skull. At that very moment a passing snake must attack the frog and try to bite it. But be careful: It must miss, and a drop of the venom it was about to inject into the frog must fall into the skull. Then you will have the remedy for your wife."

The man found it hard to believe. In that area it hardly ever rained. Snakes were rare. The astral conjunction came once in a century. And anyway, how could he place hope in an unlikely series of events such as the wise healer described? "It's all very simple, don't worry, it's easy," the healer replied.

With serious doubts the man followed instructions. After a long search, he found the skull, placed it in the desert, and

waited. It rained. Shortly after, believe it or not, a frog appeared,
then a snake, and everything went exactly as prescribed.
Once the medicine was ready, the woman drank it, and in a
trice she was cured.

—VEDANTA

This story is told in the Indian Vedanta tradition to show
that if we trust in life, it will somehow guide, support,
and enlighten us—even when we suffer, when everything seems
to go awry. In the apparent chaos of our existence, a divine plan
is secretly at work; it governs our lives from birth to death—and
that includes the hardest and most desperate moments as well.
When we perceive the world this way, we are in a true state of
grace.

It is no wonder that our reaction to such an idea is skeptical, if
not in fierce disagreement: "My son has been studying for years,
and yet he hasn't found a job," "My husband left me alone with
three children," "I have been in a wheelchair since my accident."
Where is the sense in all this? Waiting with the skull in the desert? Are you kidding? The frog does not appear, or if it does,
there is no snake, and if it ever comes, it will just mind its own
business.

But think a moment: it is precisely as the story says. We all are
improbable, in fact highly improbable. Each one of us is the result
of countless circumstances that could have been completely different. If my father had missed that train and not met my mother,

I would not exist. And if I had walked in that particular street five seconds sooner, the giant icicle would have fallen right on my head (instead of in front of me). Yet here I am. I am sure we could all play hundreds of games with such fantasies.

Actually, we live in a world much more improbable than that illustrated by the Indian story, yet can know this only *after* all is said and done. It is just because things have happened the way they have happened that the world has its own history, and that history belongs to us—even when nothing seems to work the right way. Imagine instead a world that unfolds wholly by chance: you would no longer understand anything. People would speak a thousand incomprehensible languages, as in the Tower of Babel or Dante's *Inferno*. Dante's very first impression of Hell is of a horrendous chaos, a total, unbearable lack of meaning. And if nothing had any sense, everyone's acts would be senseless gestures in a chaos without end.

Our world, however, *does* make sense. Perhaps it is our brain that gives order and meaning to the blooming, buzzing confusion. This explains the adaptive function of our ability to construct meaning: Somehow, it is much easier to survive if we invent a story and place ourselves in it. Or, one could say, the meaning is inherent to the universe. Or yet again, it is part of divine providence. These are all perfectly respectable hypotheses.

One thing is certain: meaning is a vital resource. To be able to live a life pervaded by it is a relief and a strength. In fact, people find varying degrees of meaning in their lives: a project may light their way and give them energy to forge ahead. They aim at a goal: to make money, ensure safety, be famous and admired, manage to live a few more weeks, take care of others, create a work of art, find food and water for their children before nightfall—the possibilities are endless.

Sense and nonsense are incompatible. And it is hard to conceive that a large number of senseless events produce coherent meaning. Remember the case of the monkey at a typewriter (or computer)? The hypothesis was, if the monkey were to write for a very, very long time, sooner or later it would compose *Hamlet* or the Bible (this idea has been around for a while). Someone even organized the experiment. Six monkeys at a zoo were given a computer. They looked at it suspiciously, struck it a number of times, made noises for a while, peed on it, finally pressed some keys at random—mostly the letter *s*, as the experimenters were quick to note. Then they became fed up and dropped the whole thing. No Shakespeare. Not even a haiku. I have great respect for all primates: they are magnificent animals, our closest relatives. But forget literature.

So, is there sense to our life, or does it happen by chance? Are we free or are we determined by impersonal forces? I do not wish here to address the philosophical question of whether the universe is ruled by a transcendental intelligence, whether there exists a *sense* to it, and whether, in a world that has sense, we are free or not. I wish to speak mainly of actual experiences. Sometimes we—or at least some of us—have a clear and direct understanding of a will that is greater than us: no longer a hypothesis about the nature of the universe, but a direct and self-evident perception. In this experience, (1) we feel part of a whole; (2) there is a sense of lightness and effortlessness; (3) every action, every event, takes place with a will of its own; (4) this perception is accompanied by a sense of rightness ("all is well"); (5) we have a feeling of joy and gratitude; (6) we experience a new, wider identity in which the borders of the self fall away; and (7) the events of life appear to be a guide in a story we discover bit by bit as it unfolds. This is not a run-of-the mill experience. But it happens.

If you have some familiarity with Taoism or Zen you will have recognized in my words one of the descriptions of *wu wei*, doing without doing. Alan Watts, the renowned interpreter of Eastern philosophy in the West, describes this state (which he reached through Zen meditation) thus:

> Your consciousness, your breathing, and your feelings are all the same process as the wind, the trees growing, the insects buzzing, the water flowing, and the distant prattle of the city. All this is a single many-featured "happening," a perpetual *now* without either past or future, and you are aware of it with the rapt fascination of a child dropping pebbles into a stream.

THIS EXPERIENCE VARIES GREATLY, depending on individual characteristics, context, culture, degree of intensity, and so on. Always it is felt as strongly positive and desirable, and seems to bestow a deeper and more authentic knowledge of our existence. Furthermore, all sensations of weakness or inferiority vanish. One feels 100 percent sheltered. In this state of mind, external events give the impression that they are almost guiding us: we meet the right person at the right time, a book opens our mind, a phrase heard by chance on the street points the way. Sometimes it is an improbable series of events that takes us by the hand and leads us on, as in a lucky streak or full-blown magic. People talk about it with a sense of surprise, happiness, and at times awe.

At this point a doubt may arise: Where does inner strength come from? Do we cultivate it, day after day, or do we unexpectedly receive it as a gift? Does it make any sense to act with courage, make plans, fight battles, persevere, overcome obstacles, learn self-mastery, become more autonomous? Or are we to accept our weaknesses, and just wait for the state of grace to come? In the unfolding of the human drama is there a place for our individual will, or are we simply puppets in the hands of fate, playing a script already written?

Much depends on how we see human destiny: free will or blind necessity? In recent years much has been said on the topic, because neuroscience has made some striking and controversial contributions. One is by Benjamin Libet, who in laboratory experiments asked his subjects to raise a finger when they felt like it. While this was taking place, the subjects could precisely signal the conscious act of will at the exact moment they thought it happened. At the same time Libet, using brain imaging, could see which areas of the brain were activated and, in particular, *when*.

You would expect the following sequence: mental decision to raise finger, activation (straight after) of the motor areas in the brain, and, lastly, raising of the finger. But wait. Libet found a curious fact: The brain was activated *before* the conscious decision, and about half a second later the subjects consciously decided; then they raised the finger. This means that the experimenters, watching the monitor showing the events in their subjects' brains, could know when the finger would be raised *before* the subjects themselves knew! This is to say that all our decisions are made by the brain without our knowledge, and when we believe we have made a decision, it had already been made in the intricate corridors of our brain. It is as if I were watching a train about to leave, and then just as it was leaving I mentally "decided" to make it leave, and then believed *I* had caused it to depart.

Libet's experiment, by now a classic, has been repeated in various modalities. Many see it as proof that free will does not exist: we merely have the *illusion* of free will. In short, the conscious will would seem to be an epiphenomenon, that is, a surface event with no say whatsoever in the unfolding of events.

I happen to have serious doubts about the setup of this experiment, and I would like to talk about them in some detail, because they can be useful in illustrating the fascinating complexity of this matter. First, let us think of the human subject in the experiment. Usually it is a student paid to participate in it. The experimenters ask him to raise his finger when he pleases. It is implicit that at some point he *has* to raise his finger. How do you think he would feel about *never* raising his finger? I think he feels obliged, since it is expected of him: We pay you to raise your finger. That is no big effort; what is the matter with you? Go on, do it! We are becoming impatient.

Second, it comes as no surprise that the brain shows areas where action is being prepared: You expect sooner or later to raise a finger, so your brain prepares itself for the action. If I am playing chess, my brain presumably prepares itself for making a move, because that is the rule of the game, even though my move will be a free one.

Moreover, the request was not "*Will* to raise your finger," but "Raise your finger when you feel like it," and this means that the experimenters from the outset did not recognize the will as an autonomous function, but confused it with a thought or an emotion, and this changes the entire situation. *Nomina sunt numina*, "words are gods": the way an experiment is worded can profoundly influence the experiment and how the subject experiences it. It is one thing to wait for the desire to act a certain way, another to *decide* to do it. This confusion between will (a distinct and independent faculty) and mind or emotional life is fairly common in neuroscience circles.

And why, in these experiments, do they so often ask subjects to raise a finger? I guess because it is the simplest thing. But do we really believe this can account for *all* possible acts of will? Can we equate the flexing of finger muscles with the decision to marry, the choice of where to live, what religious faith to uphold, which profession to undertake, whom to vote for in the next elections, or whether or not to set off the bomb? I think not. These are far more complex choices, in which a staggering multiplicity of factors play a part. Sometimes scientific abstraction does not adequately represent the complexity of life.

There is another fact to consider: In Libet's experiments, it was found that the subject still had the choice of veto; that is, once her brain was preparing itself for action, she could stop it voluntarily. Here we see that the decision to *not* do something can stop brain activity and hence the corresponding motor activity. The power of veto could explain our freedom of will: not in the doing, but in the stopping (after all, the ethical codes of several religions are based on vetoes: do not steal, do not kill, and so on). Last but not least, Libet himself (as opposed to the many who quote him) toward the end of his life was not at all sure the human will was determined by outside forces. He considered it an open question and hoped that our will would be shown after all to be free, to which prospect he cited a passage by Isaac Bashevis Singer:

> The greatest gift which humanity has received is free choice. It is true that we are limited in our use of free choice. But the little of free choice we have is such a great gift and is potentially worth so much, that for this itself life is worthwhile living.

I WOULD LIKE to mention another neuroscientist besides Libet who has made a marked contribution to the question of free will: Daniel Wegner. Wegner constructed an ingenious experiment in which, with the secret complicity of a collaborator, he made a subject think he was moving a cursor on a computer screen, when in reality it was the collaborator who was moving it. Yet the subject felt it was his own act. And this is precisely the nature of the will, according to Wegner: Our acts are not free, but happen independently of our will and are due to the inexorable laws of mechanics. So, how do we explain the fact that we feel them to be free acts? If I cross the street, if I choose chocolate rather than strawberry ice cream, if I make a donation to a charity, I feel those acts to be my free choice. Wegner says they are not, even though we all have the subjective impression that they are. He believes the brain places a kind of *official stamp* on our acts, acknowledging them as ours, to distinguish them from external events and acts of other people. A "cognitive sentiment" infers a mark of origin: I committed that act. It is like an administrative system, a guide to ourselves. The brain reckons with itself: I did this, you did that. Wegner's book is very detailed and his thesis is elegant and convincing. But in my view, to run an experiment with a computer, and give someone the illusion of having decided an act really performed by another is not enough to definitively ditch the idea of free will—just as the occurrence of optical illusions does not mean *all* our perceptions are illusory, only that some of them may be.

To better understand why it is important for some people to try at all costs to show that free will does not exist, we must keep in mind that for those with a scientific background, the idea of an act of will, spontaneous and by nature unpredictable, may appear a monstrosity—for two reasons: First, because the physical world proceeds according to necessary laws; we are part of the physical world, thus we, too, must follow these laws. To state the opposite is to think like charlatans or crackpots, people who hear voices or claim spirits move a table during a séance. Where does this imponderable force come from—a force that moves physical events but at the same time is not in any way part of the physical world, because it is neither visible nor measurable? (Needless to say, we are talking here in terms of classical physics. Quantum physics, which describes a probabilistic world, is another ball game.)

Second, the will is by its nature unpredictable. But those who use a scientific model are after the predictability of events, and endeavor to describe the laws that govern them. For them, admitting that an event is unpredictable and uncontrollable is an admission of defeat. Here it is worth pointing out a fact that is usually overlooked: Unpredictability has been a vital adaptive factor in our evolution. Whether we consider ourselves as prey or as predators, being unpredictable is crucial. A prey whose movements and habits are predictable is a goner; the better a predator is at surprising its prey, the more successful it will be. To be unpredictable is in our DNA.

The dilemma today's scientists are faced with has a surprising analogy in the one faced by medieval theologians. The problem was, if God is by definition omniscient, and He knows every detail since the beginning of the universe, including my every act and thought, then I have no free will, because if I had, not even God would know my next decision. But if God did not know my future, He would not be omniscient, therefore He would be limited and no longer God. Boethius, a Christian philosopher of the sixth century, cleverly resolved this problem. Imagine a circle and its center point. The circumference represents the passing of time: there we humans are born, live, feel, decide, do crossword puzzles or rob banks, and die—in the unfolding of time. There, we have the impression, correct at that level, of being able to freely choose between right and wrong. God, instead, is at the center and from there sees and knows the whole of human history, past, present, and future: it all exists in an eternal present. God knows our future actions, but at another level, which in no way interferes with our freedom. What is more, says Boethius, God perceives us in our freedom.

This distinction between two different levels is crucial, and, leaving aside theological considerations, I would like to bring it to the plane of our everyday experience. Doubtless, in our life various levels of experience come into play. For example, I am driving my car, worried about being late for an appointment with a friend. At that moment it is all I think about—whether I can find a shortcut, how fast to go without risk, how long my friend will wait before getting impatient, how to let him know I am in an area with no cell phone coverage; perhaps I am also irritated by this frenetic lifestyle, and so on. At that very moment, far from me, another person is checking traffic in a room filled with computer monitors. My car belongs to the multitude of vehicles, but the person checking the flow of traffic is not thinking about what each driver is experiencing: she is looking at the behavior of thousands of vehicles—among which is mine—and can perhaps predict subsequent bottlenecks, traffic jams, and other developments. The reality is the same, but seen from two entirely different yet legitimate points of view.

Another example: I am the father of four children, I have a persistent physical disturbance, and, after a clinical examination, I undergo a biopsy. Right after this test, but before knowing the result, I struggle with the fear of having a serious disease, and feel my very existence is in danger, so I begin to have anxious fantasies: my wife left alone, how my children will manage, my unfinished work, the suffering of my dear ones, my last months, and so forth. At that very moment a doctor is looking through the microscope at cells from my biopsy. He explores the microscopic world, where he recognizes various types of cells, their structures, deformities, and characteristics, just as one recognizes human faces distinct from one another. Looking at my biopsy, he sees that there are no pathological elements. This man, who has never met me, knows something about me that I do not yet know. Here, too, we find at play two completely different levels of one and the same reality.

Our life is made up of levels, and what is true at one level may not be true at another. Perhaps it is the same with our will. In my work I have seen many clients discover their will, perform an act of courage, cultivate persistence, make an important decision, become self-determining, find their calling: all manifestations of individual will, and decisive in the lives of those people. Such moments are moving and beautiful, and I regard it a privilege to have been able to walk with them on their path.

Without will there is no freedom, no health of mind. I can say this because I have also seen many people who are victims of external events, unable to make decisions, fearful and incapable of taking risks, not up to persevering in a project or finding independence—or else slaves of habit or negative thinking—and I have seen the devastating consequences of such states on their personalities and on those around them.

But the story does not stop here. I have also seen many people experience a state of unexpected grace, like the one described earlier—an experience in which the individual will seems suspended. It is essential to acknowledge that these experiences exist, because they are extraordinarily positive for those who have them; so it is also crucial to understand how they can be recognized and facilitated. Without deciding whether we belong to the free will party or the determinism party, we may expand our view and accept that there are both kinds of experience—much easier for a psychotherapist, for whom the raw material in the life of each unique patient is that which counts more than any other factor. A philosopher and a neuroscientist may find they have different viewpoints, especially when they think they must embrace one theory to the exclusion of another.

The concept of free will is so complex and varied that I do not for a moment believe I can give an organic and complete treatment here. I must point out, however, that two great philosophical traditions sustain two opposite points of view—while both affirming freedom. One has its origins in Aristotle's thought, and recognizes the existence of free choice and the chance for everyone to be their own principle or cause. From this perspective the highest expression of human dignity is free will. The other, found in Stoicism, sees the universe as a succession of necessary events. But in this scenario, to accept the world's necessity is itself an act of freedom, the true attitude of the wise: contrary to opposing one's destiny and stubbornly fighting against the inevitable. Meister Eckhart, the great German mystic, quoted the Stoic Seneca, who suggested accepting every event in life as the very one we have prayed for. The highest expression of this perspective was perhaps reached by Spinoza: for him, to acknowledge divine will in the necessity of events is *amor Dei intellectualis*, the intellectual love of God. In this love the human mind finds peace.

These two views seem in radical opposition. But perhaps they are not. They may just belong to two different levels. In the next, concluding chapter, we shall see how, in *The Odyssey*, Odysseus goes through a series of hardships and adventures of extraordinary difficulty before reaching the end, his return home: all thanks to his great tenacity, perseverance, self-control, and bravery. It is a beautiful story of individual will and intelligence. But it happens in a setting in which the gods interact with the world of humans, placing obstacles in their path, at other times helping them: thus Hermes gives Odysseus the *moli* herb—the antidote that will help him not to fall prey to Circe the sorceress; but Poseidon pursues him relentlessly through the terrible force of the sea, of which he is god; the goddess Ino, on the contrary, turns herself into a seagull and her flight guides Odysseus when he is shipwrecked. Athena inspires and encourages him step by step on his journey. And in any case, fate has the last word. In short, Odysseus is saved thanks to his capabilities and values in a universe that is nevertheless governed by powers higher than he: in this field, transpersonal forces with a vaster and more powerful scope than those of humans interact with one another. Homer had already resolved in poetry the apparent contradiction between freedom and necessity.

Let us now go back to the central question: What place does the will have in the art of living, and, specifically, in education and psychotherapy? In some ways free will exists and gives shape to our fate, in other ways we seem moved by laws independent of our beliefs and illusions. There are people who, in finding their capacity to will, take a stride forward, and others who, in surrendering to a greater will, find joy.

In sum, these views of life and these interpretations of the universe seem incompatible. But here the Rorschach inkblots spring to mind. In these abstract patterns the subjects may see all kinds of entities, and interpret them differently. We, too, in that great Rorschach inkblot called life, give diverse interpretations that also have diverse consequences. They may be incompatible interpretations, yet they are all legitimate, and can coexist. One point is clear: the discovery and development of the will and of inner strength are central themes of our life, and real satisfaction and happiness are impossible without the cultivation of self-discipline, the willingness to risk, the capacity for concentration and perseverance, resilience and independence.

I will explain why. Let us try the following thought experiment: Imagine that tomorrow someone discovers that free will does not exist. She manages to show it with such conclusive evidence and persuasive force that nobody would dream of contesting it and everyone actually begins to *perceive* this state of affairs. Now we really do feel like entities that move, think, feel, eat, reproduce, and sleep, subject to rigid, inexorable mechanical laws: no more, no less, than a coffee machine, a watch, or a dishwasher. Suddenly, with this new perception, all our responsibilities evaporate. We no longer stand before the choice between good and evil, truth and falsehood. Everything proceeds by itself without responding to a higher principle of freedom. How would we be, and what would our life be like? It is hard to say, maybe because this way is so strange and far from our day-to-day thinking. But let us try: every one of our acts would be arbitrary and irresponsible, and therefore unaccountable. Would you ever feel like putting a dishwasher on trial? Just so, human beings would not be answerable for any of their acts, because they could not choose otherwise. What would happen to our civilization? It could not survive as we know it. I believe that if free will did not exist, we would have to invent it.

Nevertheless, the sensation of "non-will" sometimes occurs, and that, as we have seen, can be a moment of great value. This is one of the paradoxes of human life. Here I would like to tell Gaia's story. I had guided Gaia, a student in her early twenties, through a few sessions, and helped her struggle with some important, and hard, personal decisions. She then left for South America. I asked her to send me a postcard with a phrase that would summarize what she was learning on the trip. Time passed, and then one day a postcard came: "There is no choice."

What do you mean, "There is no choice"? What about all the work we had done for her to reach a choice, in which she took her life in her own hands? On her return, Gaia explained it to me, though I believe I had already understood: she had had a wonderful trip, visited all sorts of shaman and medicine people in South America, climbed perilous paths, met extraordinary people, went from one temple to another in various powerful places that still exist on that continent. It seemed to her, on the trip, that everything proceeded by itself, without her having to stop and deliberate; each meeting, each natural event, each new idea, even each impediment, happened in an effortless flow without decisions. She did not make choices, but *discovered* them by and by, surrendering to this unfolding. Each act, each event and person, was suffused with joy and meaning. That was what "There is no choice" meant. Yet the very same Gaia realized that it was a special period, that one cannot always fly, but must also walk using her own strength. There is space in us for both orders of experience.

So, at times we may reach a spiritual state in which everything seems to happen by itself. The heavy cloak of effort, insecurity, and fear is lifted as by a miracle, and it is given to us to live some moments of our life without the force of gravity. Our self merges with the all. This is the state of grace—and thank goodness for those moments. But it would be a mistake to try to bypass altogether individual will and personal identity, which are a vital stage in our evolution. It would be a mistake not to bear in mind how much a deficit of will can turn out to be an unbearable weight for us.

It would be like wanting to go to university without having been to primary school. I fear we would flunk, and we would be sternly sent back to the ABCs.

Peak Experiences

Sometimes a state of grace, intense and unexpected, falls upon our life. A moment in which we feel lighter, and happier, when we have a flash of understanding, everything takes on new meaning. Or perhaps our consciousness expands, and so, too, our identity; at times there is a deep sense of rightness in all that happens; problems that normally harass us are forgotten as if by magic.

Moments like these (there is a great variety) are called "peak experiences" (Maslow), and those who have had them consider them highly desirable.

Exercise

Relive a peak experience—a moment or period that had particular meaning for you, when you felt you were living at a higher and more vital emotional or mental level. It need not be anything sensational. It can be a moment that just had a bit more beauty or clarity or wonder than most.

This is not only an act of remembering, but of actually reliving, re-evoking all the sensory details, all the emotional nuances.

In which ways can you anchor in your life the gifts of this experience? What can you be and do in order to preserve what you have been given?

PRACTICAL HINTS

The will cannot directly elicit a peak experience. It can create the space for it to happen, however. Our mental space is usually busy with a thousand interests and concerns—the shopping list, an appointment the next day, a phone call to make, a child's health, etc. There is no room for peak experiences: our inner world is overcrowded.

One way to create this space is to pay more attention to what is really important to us. As stated earlier, whatever we lend our attention to, we develop and strengthen. We can do this by keeping a spiritual diary, a notebook in which we write intuitions, creative ideas, spontaneous changes, coincidences, meetings with remarkable people, moments of beauty, unusual perceptions, encounters with the mysterious, states of euphoria, episodes of "flow," in which everything we do is infused with inexplicable ease and lightness.

ODYSSEY

The Story of Odysseus

T*he Odyssey* is one of the greatest adventure stories ever told. Homer, the blind poet, collected tales that were circulating in his times: stories of perseverance, of intelligence in the face of frightening difficulties, and of courage triumphant. He turned them into a masterpiece. *The Odyssey* has its source in the depths of the human soul, and tells the story of you and me.

The tale of Odysseus is the narrative of *nostos*, the return home: coming back to one's true self. Odysseus had to wander far and wide in the world, and suffer greatly, before going back to his homeland. Death hovered continually over him: "He saw many lands, met many men, suffered much mental pain, on the sea, fighting to save his and his companions' life and their safe return." But of all his company, only he would make it back.

In common parlance the word *odyssey* has come to denote even a banal undertaking that turns out to be complex, unpredictable, and full of hardships, such as a series of errands: renewing one's passport, going downtown, or even stopping at the super-market on a busy day: "It was a real odyssey!" This is after all not surprising, because our existence is an obstacle course, with big and small hurdles challenging us in ever new and amazing ways.

The world around us, often pitiless and impersonal, does not let us off lightly. Equally so, the inner world, mysterious and disturbing, is full of apparently irresistible forces: fear, desire, anguish, rage. With the precise and profound language of poetry, *The Odyssey* reaches places that are forbidden to reason. It is a map that can guide and support us, and show us how to handle hardships and gain safety.

Odysseus is usually presented as a symbol of astuteness, *metis*. But let us not forget that he also incarnates *areté*: inner strength, the capacity to turn to the good even in difficult circumstances. This is the aspect we will focus on here. He sails the seas amid storms, meets monsters, has dealings with hostile gods and dangerous creatures, challenges peril and the temptation of facile comfort, never giving up his determination to return home. And finally succeeds in reaching his goal. In ending this book, I would like to look at the stories of *The Odyssey* as a perfect illustration of the inner strength that can emerge on the arduous and risky paths of our life. You will recognize in the various episodes the themes we have previously tackled.

The Odyssey does not actually start with Odysseus, but with his son, Telemachus, "he who was born far from the battle." When his father left, he was a newborn. Now he is a callow youth, brought up without a father, and perhaps for this reason still insecure. *The Odyssey* begins with a journey within a journey: Telemachus frees himself from his mother's protection, travels in order to find out about his father's fate, leaves behind the reassuring world of his childhood, and thus becomes a man. The story of Telemachus is an echo of his distant father's story.

As for Odysseus, we know he was able to conquer Troy by devising the stratagem of the wooden horse. But after this feat, he and all the Greeks have to return home. The journey is long and dangerous. To go home is to return to oneself after having gone far away, after having been lost in the wide world. Odysseus's house is occupied by suitors, young thugs who want to persuade his wife that he is dead, so that one of them can marry her and be the king; they want to take over his palace and role. Being dispossessed of our home is a faithful image of the disempowerment we experience when our most intimate being is taken over and dominated by extraneous forces: someone or something else commanding us, making decisions for us, trying to be our master. We feel controlled by violent emotions, unmanageable urges, invasive ideas, or the pressure of other people. We are exiled from our closest ties and our own true self. It is a wearing, painful condition.

Among the first obstacles on his way home, Odysseus finds the Lotus-eaters. These are people who, eating the lotus fruit, lose themselves in a kind of passive, indolent pleasure. They live in lethargy, slaves to their weakness. The lotus is a sweet but deceptive fruit—a true drug. It has the property of inducing forgetfulness of one's true home. Odysseus is not against pleasure. As the journey proceeds, we find that he is sensitive to the beauty of women, appreciates good wine and food. But pleasure alone should not become the central principle of our life. If it becomes our one and only value, it numbs our consciousness of self. It causes regression, release from responsibility, and an empty life. Pleasure is a gift we are given, but it may become a lethal trap.

Next, Odysseus is helped by Aeolus, the master of the winds, who offers him a leather bag containing all the winds of the world—save the one he needs for returning. It all seems easy. A tailwind gently pushes the ship in the right direction—and soon enough the ship is nearing Ithaca, Odysseus's home. He already glimpses the burning home fires and prepares for his return: the embrace of his dear ones seems near. But Odysseus's companions are suspicious. They think that Aeolus's leather bag contains treasures, and that Odysseus wants to keep them all for himself. Secretly, and against his will, they open it. All hell breaks loose: the winds suddenly rush out, unleashing a violent storm. The tempest carries the ship far away. They have to start the journey over. This episode reminds us how we easily delude ourselves. In a moment of euphoria, we may think we are already there, whereas our journey just began.

The warning comes early: Do not think you will arrive so easily. Like children, we may deceive ourselves into thinking that all our tasks are easy and simple, that life conforms to our wishes. We soon find out that it is not so. As in a labyrinth, the point that seems closest to the center turns out to be farthest:

the illusion of ease turns out to be a test of our maturity. In this story, the blown-up vessel is an apt symbol of inflation, when all that we are full of is just air.

The episode of the monstrous Cyclops Polyphemus is perhaps the best known. Odysseus and his companions are imprisoned by this Cyclops—a giant and primitive creature with only one eye, who grabs Odysseus's companions one by one and eats them. With great cunning, Odysseus manages to trick him. The lesson here is, even in the most tragic of circumstances and at the hands of the toughest enemies, we must not give up and let ourselves be overpowered, but must stay clearheaded and use our intelligence. We see the invaluable capacity to remain equanimous even in the presence of thuggery and horror. This is Odysseus's scheme to get out of the cave: He first leads the Cyclops to believe his name is Nobody; then, having made him drunk, he blinds his only eye. The Cyclops screams for pain and calls for help in the middle of the night. But when his fellow creatures come to his aid, they hear him answer that Nobody has blinded him, and think he is simply having a nightmare. Odysseus manages to escape the prison of the Cyclops's cave by being "Nobody." This is a symbolic detail: to be nobody means to strip ourselves of all titles and roles. Only by doing this can we find our inner strength. To lean on our social role, past victories, external awards, and titles weakens us. To be "Nobody" means relying only on what we are.

But after he manages to get free, Odysseus makes a mistake. He is human, he is proud, and he, too, has his weaknesses. When he is back on his ship and out of range, he proudly shouts his real name to Polyphemus: I am Odysseus! This is a blunder, because Polyphemus is the son of Poseidon, who, for the sake of revenge, will be after him to the ends of the earth. Poseidon, and the seas of which he is god, represent the force of violent emotions: "the abyss of the sea, deep, frightening, dreadful." The seas are our most turbulent passions and drives, the demons which at times command us and make us say: I don't know what came over me, I was no longer in control of myself. If we want to go back home, we have to master them.

The next stage for Odysseus is the meeting with Circe, a sorceress endowed with many powers. She gracefully receives some of Odysseus's companions, then turns them into pigs. Circe represents the uncanny power of seduction. To be seduced is to lose one's freedom and identity in exchange for a little pleasure and comfort. The transformation of men into animals signifies regression to a more primitive state. Luckily the god Hermes intervenes by giving Odysseus an antidote, thanks to which he turns the obstacle into an advantage. He treats Circe with firmness, and she turns from being a sinister and untrustworthy character into the hero's greatest ally.

Circe tells Odysseus he will have to descend into Hades, the world of the dead, who are just silent, wandering shadows. This is the most terrifying of places. Here Odysseus must meet Tiresias, the only human being who, having been both woman and man during his lifetime, possesses a wisdom that death cannot erase. In Hades Odysseus also has a poignant encounter with his mother, who reveals that she died out of grief over his absence. Odysseus tries to hug her, but he embraces only air. When we die, he learns, the soul flies away like a dream. *Nekuia*, the descent into the shadowy depths of Hades, is the confrontation with our lost relationships, with the darkest and most ancient parts of ourselves, with oblivion and death. Here Odysseus comes face-to-face with the horror of nothingness.

After the netherworld the journey continues. The Sirens, who sing exquisite music, are in reality monstrous creatures who devour humans. They entice Odysseus: "Stop your ship and listen to our voice. No one has ever passed through here with his black ship without listening to our sweet song; and all go on happier and wiser." But Odysseus had thought up a strategy. He badly wanted to hear this divine music without becoming the Sirens' victim. So before reaching them he had asked his companions to tie him to the main mast. His companions must row, but with wax in their ears so as not to heed the temptation—or obey Odysseus's requests as he, lured by the Sirens, desperately asks them to stop. Knowing his own limits allows him to enjoy the music without coming to grief. Once their ship has passed through, Odysseus and his companions see the white bones of all the sailors who yielded, and were devoured. The sublime song of the Sirens represents what is powerfully irresistible, beautiful yet lethal.

Odysseus must next navigate through a perilous strait. On one side is Charybdis, a powerful, roaring, foaming whirlpool that threatens to suck the ship in; and on the other is Scylla, a monster with six heads that assails and devours sailors. Odysseus succeeds in steering his ship between the two dangers: the way of freedom is narrow; he can fall to one danger or the other. He saves himself by keeping to the center. He sees the terrible monster with six heads, each of which has three rows of teeth and howls with an eerie voice like that of a wailing child. It suddenly emerges from the waters and hurls itself at some of the men: "Scylla devoured the screaming men," Odysseus would later relate, "as they stretched out their arms to me in the fatal fight." Odysseus can do nothing for his companions, but manages to keep his self-possession and move on in spite of the deadly threats.

The survivors reach Trinacria, the island where the sacred cattle of the Sun live. They are holy animals. To kill them for food is sacrilege. But because all winds suddenly cease, Odysseus and his crew are forced to stay on the island for a long time. Their hunger increases, and so does their impatience. Odysseus's mates want to eat—they want instant gratification. They are unable to wait—and this weakness will be their end. They kill one of the sacred animals, cook it, and eat it. They choose to satisfy the urgency of their need rather than handle the discomfort of temporary hunger. Their punishment is terrible. Those who do not master their own desires cannot proceed on the journey. When the ship passes again through the strait, Charybdis, the deadly whirlpool, sucks it down, and with it all of Odysseus's companions. Only he survives, by jumping and grabbing on to a tree that hangs out from a nearby rock.

Odysseus manages to reach Ogygia, the island of the nymph Calypso. Calypso is immortal, and has the power to confer immortality. She is in love with Odysseus, and will make him immortal on the condition that he renounce going home, and remain with her. But he does not give in, and thus pays a high price. Calypso keeps him prisoner for nine years. He could have comforts, power, immortality, and a divine woman as his partner. At one stage Calypso compares herself to Penelope: what mortal woman can withstand competition with an eternally young and beautiful goddess? And yet Odysseus is strong enough to say no. He does not want to give up his wife, his son, his true home. And then, no love is authentic if you are not free. In the end the gods help him. He builds a raft and can set sail once more.

But the troubles for Odysseus are not yet over. Poseidon sends a "huge, fearful, dreadful" wave against the small craft, and shatters it. Odysseus arrives to the shore of an unknown land. Exhausted, he winds up naked on an unfamiliar beach, and without his role, his victories, his prestige, his ship, and his companions. This is point zero: everything inessential has been eliminated. Odysseus has no more support, no help. He has no props. Now he really is nobody. At certain moments in our life, all we believed in, everything we thought we were, and all that in one way or another helps and supports us, no longer counts. We are left with nothing.

Odysseus here meets the Phaeacians—a hospitable and highly cultured people. And Nausicaa, their beautiful young princess, is not afraid when she meets him in his naked, distraught state after the shipwreck, looking "like a wild boar." He is received with grace and generosity. Here, too, Odysseus could stop, but he refuses the comfort, and perhaps the chance to begin his life again in a magnificent place, marry Nausicaa, gain a position of respect and influence with his kind hosts, and perhaps one day become the king. Once more he chooses to go home.

The adventures of Odysseus are spectacular and varied. But they would be nothing if there were not someone waiting for him. There is another protagonist—silent and patient. It is Penelope, his wife. Penelope stands for the strength of holding a thought even when everything in life seems to invalidate it. She is the epitome of loyalty. For all she knows, Odysseus may have lost his way, or died on the way back, shipwrecked or killed in some other way, or maybe alive, but in some distant land and with a new family. The suitors wish to win her over. But she persists in her loyalty. Penelope shows us how to not yield to pressure, and stay faithful to ourselves.

Odysseus uses his inner strength in bravely confronting fearsome obstacles and dreadful monsters, like Scylla or Polyphemus; he does not become inflated when the goal seems near; he does not give in to flattery and seduction, as with Calypso or Circe; he does not yield to the temptation of immediate pleasure at the cost of goals that are remote, as in the episode of the Lotuseaters or the sacred cattle of the Sun; he withstands numerous hardships and trials, giving up pleasures that would make him forget his true purpose; descending to Hades, he faces the terror of nothingness. But always he is resolute in his determination to go home.

Now and then Homer tells us what happens in Odysseus's mind. His companions follow their impulses mindlessly: they are unconscious humanity, victims of their own weaknesses. Odysseus calmly deliberates on the best option, as for example when Polyphemus kills two of his companions in the cave, and he is ready to draw his sword and kill the Cyclops. But then who would shift the enormous mass blocking the exit? So he controls his impulse. Odysseus is able to decide freely even in an emergency. The whole poem represents the vicissitudes of the human soul, which must tap all resources of intelligence, resolve, and self-mastery in order to find its own fulfillment.

The final test for Odysseus is the return to his occupied home. After shrewdly preparing the trap, Odysseus acts pitilessly. The first to fall is the chief suitor, Antinous: "Odysseus aimed and struck him in the throat with a dart, the point penetrated the soft neck. So struck, he bent backward, the cup fell from his hands, a dense blood spurted from his nostrils." The others fall one by one. Odysseus takes back his kingdom, his power, his dignity. He is at last ready to find the other half of himself, his woman, who for twenty years has waited for him. The two poles, masculine and feminine, are reunited, and this means the fullness of being, conquered through countless trials by courage, tenacity, and the intelligent will.

According to Joseph Campbell's precise interpretation Odysseus and Penelope are the sun and the moon, who meet at the end of every twenty-year cycle, at the time of the winter solstice (the new sun and new moon). The meeting between sun and moon is the cosmic union: a wholeness in which time stands still and we can at last find peace.

References

INTRODUCTION

Alberti, A. *Psicosintesi. Una cura per l'anima.* Firenze: L'Uomo Edizioni, 2008.

Assagioli, R. *The Act of Will.* New York: Viking, 1973.

Bonacina, P. *Manuale di psicosintesi.* Milano: Xenia, 2010.

Brown, D. E. *Human Universals.* New York: McGraw-Hill, 1991.

Griffin, D. *Animal Minds: Beyond Cognition to Consciousness.* Chicago, IL: University of Chicago Press, 2011.

Guggisberg Nocelli, P. *La via della psicosintesi.* Firenze: L'Uomo Edizioni, 2011.

Sarkissian, H., Chatterjee, A., De Brigard, F., et al. "Is Belief in Free Will a Cultural Universal?" *Mind & Language* (June 2010), 25(3): 346–358.

Sawyer, G. J., and Deak, V. *The Last Human.* New Haven, CT: Yale University Press, 2007.

FREEDOM

Baumeister, R. F., Vohs, K. D., DeWall, C. N., and Zhang, L. "How emotions shape behavior: feedback, anticipation and reflection rather than direct causation," *Personality and Social Psychology Review* (November 2007): 167–203.

Baumeister, R. F., Masicampo, E. J., and De Wall, C. N. "Prosocial Benefits of Feeling Free: Disbelief in Free Will Increases Aggression and Reduces Helpfulness," *Personality and Social Psychology Bulletin* (February 2009), 35(2): 260–268.

Berlin, I., trans. H. Hardy. *Liberty.* Oxford: Oxford University Press, 2002.

Brembs, B. "Towards a scientific concept of free will as a biological trait: spontaneous actions and decision-making in invertebrates," *Proceedings of the Royal Society: Biological Sciences* (December 15, 2010).

Crick, F. *The Astonishing Hypothesis.* New York: Simon & Schuster, 1995.

Farahany, N. A. "A Neurological Foundation for Freedom." *Stanford Technology Law Review* (2012), 4.

———. "Searching Secrets." *University of Pennsylvania Law Review* (April 2012) 160(5).

Haggard, P. "Decision time for free will," *Neuron* (February 10, 2011), 69(3): 404–406.

REFERENCES

Juth, N., and Lorentzon, F. "The concept of free will and forensic psychiatry," *International Journal of Law and Psychiatry* (January–February 2010), 33(1): 1–6.

Kane, R. *A Contemporary Introduction to Free Will*. New York: Oxford University Press, 2005.

Langer, J. E. "Long-Term Effects of a Control-Relevant Intervention with the Institutionalized Aged," *Journal of Personality and Social Psychology* (1977), 35(12): 897–902.

Mackintosh, N., et al. "Neuroscience and the Law," *The Royal Society* (December 2011), DES2420.

Marmot, M. G., Bosma, H., Hemingway, H., et al. "Contribution of job control and other risk factors to social variations in coronary heart disease incidence," *Lancet* (July 26, 1997), 350 (9073): 235–239.

Marmot, M. G., Rose, G., Shipley, M., et al. "Employment grade and coronary heart disease in British civil servants," *Journal of Epidemiology and Community Health* (1978), 32 (4): 244–249.

Mele, A. R. *Effective Intentions—the Power of Conscious Will*. New York: Oxford University Press, 2009.

Rigoni, D., Kuhn, S., Sartori, G., et al. "Inducing disbelief in free will alters brain correlates of preconscious motor preparation: The brain minds whether we believe in free will or not," *Psychological Science* (2011), 22: 613–618.

Roskies, A. "How Does Neuroscience Affect Our Conception of Volition?" *Annual Review of Neuroscience* (2010), 33: 109–130.

———. "Neuroscientific Challenges to Free Will and Responsibility," *Trends in Cognitive Sciences*, 10(9).

Rumi. *The Paragon Parrot*. London: Watkins Publishing, 2002.

Spence, S., and Firth, C. "Towards a Functional Anatomy of Volition" in Libet, B., Freeman, A., and Sutherland, K. *The Volitional Brain: Towards a Science of Free Will*. Exeter: Imprint Academic Exeter, 2004.

Spinney, Laura. "Blink, and you live—doctor's message to man in a coma," *The Guardian*, April 14, 2004.

Vohs, K. D., and Schooler, W. J. "The Value of Believing in Free Will," *Psychological Science*, 19(1): 49–54.

THE CENTER

Assagioli, Roberto. *The Act of Will*. New York: Viking, 1973.

Beauregard, M., Lévesque, J., and Bourgoin, P. "Neural Correlates of Conscious Self-regulation of Emotion," *Journal of Neuroscience* 21 (2001): RC165 (1–6).

Beauregard, M., and O'Leary, D. *The Spiritual Brain*. New York: HarperCollins, 2007.

Bhagavad Gita. Translated by S. Radhakrishnan. New York: Harper & Row, 1973.

Plato. *The Republic*. Translated by Desmond Lee. London: Penguin Classics, 2007.

Piazza, J. R., Charler, S. T., Sliwinski, M. J., et al. "Affective Reactivity to Daily Stressors and Long-Term Risk of Reporting a Chronic Physical Health Condition," *Annals of Behavioral Medicine* (February 2013), 45(1): 110–120.

Read Macdonald, M. *Peace Tales*. Atlanta, GA: August House, 1992.

Schwartz, J., and Gladding, R. M. *You Are Not Your Brain*. New York: Avery, 2011.

Schwartz, J. M., and Begley, S. *The Mind and the Brain*. New York: Regan Books, 2002.

Siegel, D. J. *Mindsight*. Melbourne: Scribe, 2009.

WILL

Asbjornsen, P. C., and Moe, J. *Norwegian Folktales*. New York: Pantheon, 1982.

Bandura, A. *Self-efficacy*. New York: W. H. Freeman and Company, 1997.

Baumeister, R. *Willpower*. New York: Penguin, 2011.

Oaten, M., and Cheng, K. "Longitudinal Gains in Self-regulation from Regular Physical Exercise," *British Journal of Health Psychology* (2006), 11: 717–733.

Troutwine R., and O'Neal, E. C. "Volition, performance of a boring task and time estimation," *Perceptual and Motor Skills* (June 1981), 52(3): 865–866.

PLASTICITY

Bucay, J. *Lascia che ti racconti*. Milano: Rizzoli, 2004.

Cramer, S. C., et al. "Harnessing neuroplasticity for clinical applications," *Brain* (June 2011), 134(6): 1591–1609.

Farid ud-Din Attar, trans. C. S. Nott. *The Conference of the Birds*. London: Routledge & Kegan Paul, 1954.

Kandel, E. *In Search of Memory*. Norton: New York, 2006.

Kircher, T., et al. *Biological Psychiatry* (August 23, 2012).

Olsson, C. J. "Imaging Imagining Actions," Department of Integrative Medical Biology, Section for Physiology, Umeå University (2008).

Robertson, I. *Mind Sculpture*. London: Bantam, 1999.

MASTERY

Allen, D. *Getting Things Done*. London: Piatkus, 2011.

Bhagavad Gita. Translated by S. Radhakrishnan. New York: Harper & Row, 1973.

Cheung-Blunden, V. *Delay of Gratification*. Berkeley, CA: VDM, 2009.

Csikszentmihaly, M. *Flow: the Psychology of Optimal Experience*. New York: Harper & Row, 1990.

deCharms, R., *Personal Causation*. New York: Academic Press, 1968.

Erdoes, R., and Ortiz, A. *American Indian Myths and Legends*. New York: Pantheon, 1984.

Mischel, W., Shoda, Y., and Rodriguez, L. "Delay of Gratification in Children," *Science* (May 1989), 244(4987): 933–938.

Moffitt et al. "A Gradient of Self-Control, Predicts Health, Wealth, and Public Safety," *Proceedings of the National Academy of Sciences* (January 24, 2011).

Muravena, M. "Building self-control strength: Practicing self-control leads to improved self-control performance," *Journal of Experimental Social Psychology* (March 1, 2010), 46(2): 465–468.

Quinn, J., Pascoe, A., Wood, W., et al. "Can't Control Yourself? Monitor Those Bad Habits," *Personality and Social Psychology Bulletin* (March 2010), 46(2): 465–468.

AUTONOMY

Deci, E. *Why We Do What We Do*. New York: Penguin Books, 1996.

Dweck, C. *Mindset: The New Psychology of Success*. New York: Ballantine, 2007.

Eliade, M. *Images et symboles*. Paris: Gallimard, 1952.

———. *Mythes, reves et mystères*. Paris: Gallimard, 1957.

Emerson, R. W., trans. P. Pignata. *La fiducia in se stessi*. Pavia: Ibis, 2012.

Stallibrass, A. *The Self-Respecting Child*. Cambridge, MA: Da Capo Press, 1982.

RESILIENCE

Duckworth, A., Peterson, C., Matthews, M., et al. "Grit: Perseverance and Passion for Long-Term Goals," *Journal of Personality and Social Psychology* (2007), 92(6): 1087–1101.

Haidt, J. *The Happiness Hypothesis*. London: Arrow Books, 2006.

Reich, J. W., Zautra, A. J., and Hall, S. H., eds. *Handbook of Adult Resilience*. New York: Guilford Press, 2010.

Seligman, M.E.P. *Flourish*. New York: Free Press, 2011.

Taleb, M. N. *Antifragile*. London: Penguin Books, 2012.

Wolin, S. J., and Wolin, S. *The Resilient Self*. New York: Villard, 1993.

DEPTH

Chuang Tzu. *The Complete Works of Chuang Tzu*. New York: Columbia University Press, 1968.

Ericsson, A. *The Road to Excellence*. Hillsdale, NJ: Lawrence Erlbaum Associates, 1996.

Farid ud-Din Attar, trans. C. S. Nott. *The Conference of the Birds*. London: Routledge & Kegan Paul, 1954.

Howe, M.J.A. *Genius Explained*. Cambridge: Cambridge University Press, 1999.

Marlys, Mayfield. *Thinking for Yourself: Developing Critical Thinking Skills Through Reading and Writing*. Belmont, CA: Wadsworth, 1994.

Marton, F. "On Qualitative Differences in Learning—2: Outcome as a function of the learner's conception of the task," *British Journal of Education. Psych*, 46: 115–127.

Oberman, S., and Schram, P. *Solomon and the Ant*. Honesdale, PA: Boyds Mills Press, 2006.

Shenk, D. *The Genius in All of Us*. New York: Anchor Books, 2011.

Zhuang-zi. *a cura di Liou Kia-Hway*. Milano: Adelphi, 2010.

INTEGRITY

Bartal, I. B., Decety, J., and Mason, M. "Empathy and Pro-Social Behavior in Rats," *Science* (December 9, 2011), 334(6061): 1427–1430.

Brosnan, S. F. "Fair Refusal by Capuchin Monkeys," *Nature* (March 2004), 428(11).

Henrich, J., et al., "Markets, Religion, Community Size, and the Evolution of Fairness and Punishment," *Science* (March 19, 2010), 327: 1480–1484.

Hulnik, H. R., and Hulnik, M. R. *Loyalty to Your Soul*. New York: Hay House, 2011.

Monroe, K. R., Martin, A., and Ghosh, P. "Politics and an Innate Moral Sense Scientific Evidence for an Old Theory?" *Political Research Quarterly* (September 2009), 62(3): 614–634.

Nichols, S. *Sentimental Rules*. New York: Oxford University Press, 2004.

Schwartz, H. *Leaves from the Garden of Eden*. New York: Oxford University Press, 2009.

Sommers, T. *Relative Justice*. Princeton, NJ: Princeton University Press, 2012.

Sommerville, J. A., Schmidt, M.F.H., and Yun, J., et al. "The Development of Fairness Expectations and Prosocial Behavior in the Second Year of Life," *Infancy* (2013), 18(1): 40–66.

Tullett, A. M., and Inzlicht, M. "The voice of self-control: blocking the inner voice increases impulsive responding." *Acta Psychologica* (Amst.) (October 2010), 135(2): 252–256.

Vale, L. J., and Campanella, T., eds. *The Resilient City*. New York: Oxford University Press, 2005.

Waley, A. *Three Ways of Thought in Ancient China*. London: George Allen & Unwin, 1969.

COURAGE

Bhagavad Gita. Translated by S. Radhakrishnan. New York: Harper & Row, 1973.

Levenson, M. "Risk Taking and Personality," *Journal of Personality and Social Psychology* (1990), 58(6): 1073–1080.

Pury, C.L.S., and Lopez, S.J., eds. *The Psychology of Courage*. Washington, DC: American Psychological Association, 2010.

Scheubb, H. *African Tales*. Madison, WI: University of Wisconsin Press, 2005.

Schiller, D. "Snakes in the MRI Machine: A Study of Courage," *Scientific American* (July 20, 2010): 24.

Trimpop, R. *The Psychology of Risk-Taking Behavior*. Amsterdam: Elsevier Science, 1994.

THE STATE OF GRACE

Damasio, A. *Self Comes to Mind*. New York: Pantheon Books, 2010.

Dennett, D. *Intuition Pumps and Other Tools of Thinking*. New York: Norton, 2013.

Frith, C. *Making up the Mind*. Malden, MA: Blackwell, 2007.

Gazzaniga, M. *Who's in Charge?* New York: HarperCollins, 2011.

Haynes, J. D., et al, "Unconscious determinants of free decisions in the human brain," *Nature Neuroscience* (2008), 11: 543–545.

Kandel, E. *The Age of Insight*. New York: Random House, 2012.

Kindler, B. B. *Sri Ramakrishna's Stories*. Honokaa: Sarada Ramakrishna Vivekananda Association, 2002.

Minsky, M. *The Society of Mind*. New York: Simon & Schuster, 1985.

Pearce, M.S.J. *Free Will?* Ginger Prince Publications, 2010.

Watts, A. *In My Own Way*. New York: Pantheon, 1972.

Wegner, D. M. *The Illusion of Conscious Will*. Cambridge, MA: MIT Press, 2002.

ODYSSEY: THE STORY OF ULYSSES

Homer, *The Odyssey*. Translated by R. Fagles. New York: Penguin Classics, 1997.

Acknowledgments

Writing this book has been a wonderful but arduous journey. I had to develop a good deal of persistence and determination. I rediscovered the will in writing about the will.

In this adventure I have had help from many people: Roberto Assagioli first introduced me to the theme of the will. My wife, Vivien, as always, has given me excellent ideas—and what a phenomenal advantage it is to have an in-house translator! My students and patients have been an inexhaustible source of inspiration. My publisher, Mitch Horowitz, has given me advice that has greatly improved the book. David Koral's precise and sensitive editing has significantly improved the text.

To all of them: a huge, grateful thank-you.

Index

Enigma of Time exercise, 102–4
Ericsson, K. Anders, 133
escapism, 109
ethics. *See* integrity
Ethiopian story on courage, 187–88
Evoking Courage exercise, 204–6
evolution
    brain structures and functions, 34–35,
        191–92
    capacity for will and free choice, 13, 59,
        225
    cultivation of inner strength, xxii
    group membership and support, 14, 107,
        195
    resilience in, xxi
    risk-taking, 190, 191–92
    self-mastery, 102
    sense of justice, 169, 172
    unpredictability as adaptive factor in, 217
exercises
    Art of Reflection, 142–44
    Being, 45–47
    Breathing, xxiii–xxv
    Changing Perspective, 159–61
    Creating a World, 84–86
    Enigma of Time, 102–4
    Evoking Courage, 204–6
    Guiding Star, 183–85
    Inventory of Resources, 121–23
    Peak Experiences, 225–27
    Silence, 23–25
    Training the Will, 62–65
explanatory styles, 156
extrinsic and intrinsic motivation, 113–16

failure. *See* mistakes and failure; risk
Farid ud-Din Attar, 136–38
fatalism and passivity, 17–18, 53–54,
    212–17
fear. *See also* courage; risk
    brain structures involved, 191–92
    directing attention to, 73–74
    disidentification from, 36
    excessive caution and missed
        opportunities, 192–93

exercise for exploration of, 64
of freedom and choice, 4, 11
manipulation of fears of others, 14
means to overcome, 200
of responsibility, 4, 11, 22, 150–51
sword of Damocles allegory, 193
withdrawal of attention from, 79–80
Finnish story on autonomy, 105–6
flow, experience of, 100–101
Foix-Chavany-Marie syndrome, 19
forgiveness, 180–81
freedom of will. *See also* will
    belief in, 19–22
    brain-machine interaction, 17
    ceding of decisions to others, 10–11
    within civilized society, 6–9
    in daily acts, xvi, 22
    evolution of capacity for, 13, 59, 225
    as expression of human dignity, 221
    as expression of identity, 4, 6
    fear of, 4, 11, 22
    as gift, 215
    in Greek mythology, 5–6
    health benefits of making decisions,
        12–13
    as illusion, 17–18, 213, 216–17
    limitations and degrees of independence,
        5, 83–84, 215
    locked-in syndrome, 16
    manipulation by others, 13–15
    moment of decision, 15
    neuroscientific studies on, 212–16
    ownership of life, 15–16
    Rumi on, 1–2, 22
    self-efficacy, 22
    Silence exercise, 23–25
    Stoic acceptance of necessary events, 221
    suffering through constraint of, 2–4, 231
    as theological question, 217–18
    unpredictability, 4, 9
    voluntary versus involuntary action,
        8–9, 18–19, 33–35
    as way of being, 22–23
free play, 116
future-orientation, 152

About the Author

PIERO FERRUCCI is a psychotherapist and philosopher. He has been a student of and collaborator with Roberto Assagioli, the founder of psychosynthesis. His books include *The Power of Kindness, What We May Be, Inevitable Grace, Beauty and the Soul,* and *What Our Children Teach Us.* He lives in Florence, Italy.